Blowing the Whistle
on Intercollegiate Sports

Blowing the Whistle

on

Intercollegiate

Sports

J. Robert Evans

 Nelson-Hall Company, Chicago

ISBN: 0-911012-94-x

Library of Congress Catalog Card Number: 74-78842

Manufactured in the United States of America.

Library of Congress Cataloging in Publication Data

Evans, J Robert.
 Blowing the whistle on intercollegiate sports.

 1. College sports. I. Title.
 GV347.E82   796.33'263'0973   74-78842
 ISBN 0-911012-94-X

Contents

What's the Problem?

What's new on today's college campuses? In a few words, the left-wingers have become less outwardly active but just as negative, the solemn aftermath of Kent State and the campus violence of the late sixties still cast a shadow of gloom upon the faces of today's students, casual clothes are the rule, no longer the exception, pot thrives as the collegiate cure for hypocrisy, and big-time college athletics are threatened with sliding down the gymnasium laundry chute with about as much dignity as yesterday's dirty towels.

To collegiate sports fans though, the plight of the activist, the onset of wild clothes, and the increasing use of pot on today's campuses ironically seems unimportant when compared to the steady decline of the holy sanctuary of college athletics. "Is it possible," sports fans are asking, "that the hubbub and hip-hurrah of college sports are dwindling and maybe even

1

dying? Isn't it important that college athletics survive?" "For what?" a sports critic may retort. "Well," the sports fan will probably reply, "because they're part of America, they represent the American way." "So does prostitution and payola," the critics may argue. So begins another endless debate. But, the fallout of the original premise remains—the multi-million dollar collegiate sports industry may be approaching ruin.

College sports not only face financial problems and some ethical ones too, but more important, for the first time ever, they face the emergence of a doubting public. Doubting the very importance and necessity of big-time college sports. That, sports fans, is some kind of problem.

If this trend continues, the heretofore sacred but overgrown cow of college athletics may be slaughtered and used to feed the needy natives. Translated, that means the money, prestige, and effort previously devoted to college sports will be reappropriated and used in more meaningful ways elsewhere.

Primarily, students would prefer the money and effort be spent to support other university activities such as intramural and club sports, day care centers, world peace-oriented groups, public speaker forums, assistance to community welfare groups, and the like.

Several persistent problems plague college sports and threaten to ruin them. First is the reluctance of students to support athletics. At the University of California at Berkeley, for example, students voted 1,763 to 1,238 to recommend the $300,000 stipend they annually give to help support Cal's athletic program be reallocated and used in a manner more representative of all students. Not only did the students'

vote go against their continued financial support of
athletics at Cal, but the issue was of such little interest
to the students that only approximately 3,000 voted
out of a student body of more than 20,000 students.

"How ungrateful," it was probably whispered by
the Berkeley sports hierarchy, "for those radicals to
really care about how they spend their own money."
Care is just what they did. "How important is a sports
program?" the students most likely asked themselves.
"Who benefits, and to whom else or where else could
the money and effort be allocated more appropriately?"

Thoughts such as these are no longer just pon-
dered by students; they are dropped like bombs right
on the 50-yard line.

The Berkeley example is not an isolated case.
Similar situations have occurred at large universities
nationwide. At the University of California in San
Diego a few years back, the students nixed the
school's one-year-old financial aid-to-athletes arrangement and, most probably, any chances the
university had of going big-time athletically. This they
did by approving the following referendum by an as-
tounding 75 percent:

The U.C.S.D. Campus Policy concerning financial aid to athletes should be the result of con-
sultation with all members of the U.C.S.D.
academic community. However, because the
results of this policy decision will most directly
affect the students, and because the intercollegiate athletic program is run exclusively for the
benefit of the students, the students' opinion, as
represented by the results of this referendum,

should be of paramount importance in determining the campus policy with respect to financial aid to athletes.

The current policy administers grants-in-aid to students in need with no special consideration for athletes. Should this existing policy be amended in the following way?

Should some special financial assistance (drawn exclusively from private sources) be awarded to athletes irrespective of their need?

yes _____   no _____

Students at Ohio University, a reputed hotbed of college sports, went a step further than just voting against aid to athletes. They voted to recommend the abolishment of all collegiate sports except basketball. Basketball was exonerated only because construction had just been completed on the school's $12 million basketball arena.

The second problem pushing big-time athletics toward obscurity is that coaches are accused of being dictators and of building little empires—all at the expense of the athletes. Coaches are being chided for demanding that athletes adhere to unreasonably stiff disciplinary and behavior codes. Oregon State's football coach, Dee Andros, admiringly called the "Great Pumpkin," became the symbol of these alleged "unreasonable" disciplinary demands, when national news media publicized an ultimatum he issued to his players to eliminate their beards and/or mustaches or face expulsion from the team. Andros, however, was not alone in his feelings and his problems. Football coaches Rudy Feldman, at the University of New Mexico, and Woody Hayes, at Ohio State, in addition to several other big name coaches face similar dilemmas.

Thirdly, athletic finances have soared. They are approaching the point at which they alone may force the abolition of collegiate sports. At the University of California at Los Angeles the total athletic budget has reached an astronomical $2.3 million annually and that does not include the money alumni and friends throw in the hopper to help out the athletic program. Georgia Institute of Technology has a similar problem. Its total athletic budget has climbed to approximately $2.5 million a year.

UCLA and Georgia Tech are not lone rangers in their battles with the budget. Every big-time collegiate athletic program in the country has a million-dollar-plus budget—more to the plus than the million-dollar side. Some schools have begun to answer their budget problems, though. Alabama, for instance, has cut out its annual shrimp dinner for high school coaches prior to home games. Now, that may sound like an absurd budget cut but in Alabama where football games seem more important than school integration, that truly is a large cut. The University of Illinois is doing its thing for the economy too. It no longer buys a complete new set of uniforms every season. Don't laugh—at least it's a start.

Fourthly, racism charges have been leveled against many big-time sports programs. Mormon-operated Brigham Young University has been one of the schools that has been hit the hardest by this problem. They suffered through two football seasons of cancelled games and demonstrations because of the Mormon Church's alleged racist policies. Even Johnny Wooden, UCLA's basketball coach, the pagan idol of the nation's high school basketball coaches, has had unpublicized racial problems during some of his plush years. Although the charges were leveled more against the UCLA basketball system than against Wooden himself, they, nonetheless, received acclaim. These problems first appeared when Kareem Abdul Jabbar (then, Lew Alcindor), publicized his name change as a result of his switch to the Muslim religion. religion.

Other universities, such as the University of Washington, whose racial situation is discussed in detail in this book, the University of Iowa, and San Jose State, have had racial problems related to their athletic programs. The situation at Iowa and San Jose reportedly stemmed from accusations by black athletes that they were being verbally ridiculed by the coaches, stacked in particular positions to avoid the fielding of predominantly black starting lineups, and that new blacks were not being recruited because they had been dubbed troublemakers.

There are, however, some changes taking place. Several teams in the deep South now have several black players on their rosters, which definitely is a giant step forward for the South and for big-time athletics' racial problems.

Bradley University's basketball coach, Joe Stowell, is not convinced that the problem is close to a solution though. He recently said, "Take schools like Jacksonville and Houston . . . they used to call kids 'nigger' and now they are recruiting them. . . ."

Lastly, accusations that several big-time athletic powers are illegally recruiting athletes and misrepresenting their athletic scholarships (free rides) have risen again lately. Generally, stories about under-the-table payments to stars and potential stars make up the majority of these accusations and have surfaced in the form of rumors rather than facts due to the difficulty of pinning down actual happenings. Nonetheless, the stories are usually rather accurate representations of the facts.

The problem of misrepresentation, illegal recruiting, and payment of athletes isn't a new one for big-time college athletics, though. Gymnasium walls have echoed with similar cries ever since the humble beginning of collegiate sports back in the 1860s. Nevertheless it represents another one of college athletic's current ills.

"If intercollegiate sports really does suffer from all these publicized ills," one may ask, "how can sports fans sit in front of the tube on a Saturday afternoon and listen to the game announcers praise and sanctify the merits of college sports on the Game of the Week and not be bothered by the fact that these problems may soon burst the proverbial bubble of collegiate sports?" The reply is simple, friends. Problems such as the ones college sports are presently experiencing only occur in real life, and sports fans aren't ready to face the fact that college sports may be part of the work-a-day, pay-your-bills, real world.

Television and Madison Avenue, are, in part responsible for this sham. They have sold college sports as something quite unreal. On TV, college sports exist as if in a fairyland of good guys and good deeds—where the sun never sets and the good guys always win (maybe they don't win every game but we're brainwashed by the media to think the players all win by being exposed to the "great virtues of athletics"). Sorry to say, but there is a real life for college sports and it's easy to identify too. Because reality is anywhere that it costs $750,000 to finance a football team's education for four years, where $25,000 is the low estimate for the telephone tab for one university to recruit athletes, and where rumors of professional sports teams paying the bill for college athletes' scholarships have become so common that they're hard to refute.

Nevertheless, only a few athletic programs have hung up their spikes to date. There may still be hope for collegiate athletics. College sports, with all their problems, still retain the beauty of allowing young and old, rich and poor, hippies and straight people, and fathers and sons to communicate on the same wave length—no small chore these days. College sports, whether one is a participant or spectator, allow people to forget their hang-ups and concentrate on a common cause—the game. The task for sports people then, is to save collegiate athletics. This can be done by allowing the present big-time college athletic programs to self-destruct and by cultivating the real beauty of sports through construction of a new athletic setup. Effort should be made to make the new one meaningful to the people for whom it is intended—the students. And it is with that aim in mind that this book was written.

This brief introduction to big-time intercollegiate athletics did not discuss every charge currently being levied against college sports programs, such as, the misuse of athletic scholarships, athletic isolationism, and the charge that college athletic programs have become a minor league for professional sports. Nevertheless, these issues and others are important, and they will be discussed in greater detail in subsequent sections of this book.

For now, though, let this section be ended with a definition of an athletic machine. A collegiate athletic machine is any sports program whose prime objectives are winning games; getting more money for more scholarships, more prestigious schedules, and more publicity; and producing more professional stars. Of course, these aren't publicly listed as the program's goals, but in the minds of its coaches and athletic directors they're at the top of the list.

Although it is generally assumed so, football and basketball are not the only sports with athletic machines even though they are usually its mainstays. Because they are most often the biggest sports they usually pay the freight for all the others in the schools' athletic programs. Thus, if they aren't publicized and promoted so they can draw big gates and more money, the whole program suffers financially.

Athletic machines have some other dubious trademarks too. They constantly strive to grow bigger, although not necessarily better. At least, "better" as described by most rational, educationally oriented people. As a result of this misdirected growth, machines have little concern for their players. In fact, the players usually serve as a means to their end; namely, winning at any cost.

Athletic machines are also known for their active recruiting. Machine athletes, regardless of their university's geographical location, come from coast to coast and are all under contract—more aptly named "full [or free] rides," which means they are paid to produce and win. The persisting philosophy among machine officials seems to be that if the players happen to pick up a degree along the way, they're lucky. But that's rather unimportant to the machine. More generally, their badge of excellence is not a college degree along the way, but the signing of a pro contract after serving a four-year machine internship.

Machines don't develop and grow by accident though—they are the products of overzealous coaches' and athletic directors' dreams of grandeur. And they are spoon-fed to full maturity by an overabundance of publicity, eager beaver boosters, and devious alumni.

For example, the University of Miami in Florida recently employed a professional advertising agency to promote its program. Since football attendance at the University of Miami had dwindled to an average of thirty thousand in 1971 and since receipts from football support the entire athletic program, on a big-time scale of course, Miami's athletic hierarchy and its supporters engaged the ad agency to give their product greater market appeal.

Most machines exist at large universities whose athletic budgets often exceed $1 million a year and whose athletic teams are listed as "major college" by the NCAA (National Collegiate Athletic Association), although small college programs with big-time dreams can also suffer from the machine mania too.

In short, athletic machines are collegiate sports programs that are emphasized far beyond their need, and whose emphasis is on entertaining rather than providing a learning activity for the schools' students.

Financing Collegiate Athletics

Denver University, once a big-time football power, could no longer afford to compete as one of collegiate football's biggies, so its stadium was torn down and the football money allocated to other more appropriate sources. The University of Detroit did likewise when its annual football loss approximated $60,000 a year. The University of Buffalo, facing a $100,000 deficit, saw the same light and followed suit in 1970, as did Bradley University with a $600,000 athletic debt. The University of California at Santa Barbara followed this parade in 1971, citing losses of $80,000 per year. Eighteen other schools have done likewise during the past five years. Other universities will no doubt be forced to join this parade unless the rising costs of supporting big athletic programs, particularly football and basketball, are not drastically curtailed to a sensible level.

Higher education is no small-time operator these days. In most states its costs run well into the nine figure category, $650 million for the State of Illinois, for example. It's no wonder then that the voters who are footing the bill for higher education are saying, "let's cut costs." Usually cuts and their ensuing austerity programs brought on by such cries haven't affected the holy sanctuaries of college athletics. Alas, times are changing. Now football and basketball get their budgets trimmed right along with the other guys, like the debate club, science laboratories, and dormitory additions. And it's only logical too. Athletics often account for a sizeable chunk of a university's total budget. Consider this example: If $2 million of a school's yearly budget of $25 million is spent to support an athletic program that involves only five hundred students of the school's total population of twenty thousand (which aren't unrealistic figures), that means 8 percent of the university's funds for a fiscal year are spent to operate a program in which 2.4 percent of the students participate. You answer the questions: Is that justifiable in today's tight economy? And, shouldn't the athletic program receive budget cuts along with every other part of the university?

That doesn't mean that some athletic programs aren't self-supporting and that they all depend upon revenue from their university's operating budget. Jess Hill, USC's former athletic director, although refusing to give any details, says that Southern Cal's program draws little or no income from the regular university budget and still runs in the black. USC receives most of its income from gate receipts, booster club funds, alumni contributions, and TV rights. Louisiana State University is in a similar position. Their athletic program has produced large profits over the past few years and has not drawn any of its income from the university's budget.

USC and LSU are lucky. Most other big-time collegiate sports powers receive their money from similar sources too (gate receipts, booster club funds, alumni contributions, TV and radio rights, and even from the general university budget) but don't come close to operating in the black. The University of Florida netted over $1.1 million from its football gate in 1969 and even then its total athletic program racked up an $80,000 deficit for the year. The University of Minnesota has similar money problems. Recent losing football teams have caused their average football gate to drop by $15,000 and as a result, they were anticipating an athletic deficit of $400,000 by the summer of '72.

A Big Eight Conference spokesman echoed the same sad tale. He said that half of his conference's schools face unbalanced budgets, even though they draw their income from several sources other than their universitys' budgets. Although the Big Eight is made up of schools like Nebraska, Oklahoma, and Colorado, it is currently the most prestigious football conference in the country.

Villanova University is another of those suffering from athletic budget woes. The school's football program produced a $314,000 deficit for the 1971 season, and as if that wasn't enough, Villanova students are beginning to cry for dissolution of the football program so the money can be allocated to more worthwhile purposes.

The University of Cincinnati has budget problems too. Their athletic costs doubled in the last ten years and their revenues haven't kept pace, primarily because their football team is a loser at the gate. George Smith, Cincinnati's athletic director, does point out one bright light in their otherwise dim financial picture though—the swimming team is making money at the gate. They cleared $1,000 last season which, of course, doesn't ease the athletic financial burden much.

There are several sources of revenue that are tapped to support athletics other than gate receipts and the regular university budget, such as booster club and alumni contributions. However, gate receipts are the most prominent and bring in the most money. As a result, the big-timers have arrived at several methods of splitting the game gate-pots so both opponents benefit and survive.

One of these methods is for the two competing teams to split the gate receipts evenly, after the home team skims its expenses (approximately 10 to 15 percent of the gross) off the top, of course. In an interesting comment concerning such a gate receipt contract arrangement, Clemson's football coach, Frank Howard, said he has brought his team to Georgia Tech several times over the last two decades and has returned the loser ten times, "but that $100,000 check (from a split of the gate) sure eased the pain."

Another form of contract is the flat fee type; called a *guarantee.* The visiting team is guaranteed a certain amount of the take, quite often from $20,000 to $100,-000, depending on the team's prestige and draw potential.

Then there is the contract that allows the visiting team a certain amount of tickets to sell at a certain rate, plus a guaranteed fee. For example, the visiting team may get 10,000 tickets to sell at $6.00 apiece ($60,000), in addition to a $20,000 guarantee for a total of $80,000.

There are several combination forms of these contract types too, such as the option type which gives the visiting team either a set guarantee or 50 percent of the gate, whichever is the greatest. For the most part, however, the guarantee contract remains the most popular because it sets a specific figure which makes budgeting easier.

As previously mentioned, some schools' athletic programs still rely on the receipt of a good portion of their athletic money from their universities' regular budgets which are usually appropriated by the state legislatures. Schools in this position wish to continue the practice because of the financial advantage of such an arrangement. The universities' athletic departments don't have to depend too heavily upon big crowds and gate receipts to keep their programs going. Thus, their checkbooks balance easier. Nevertheless, they are more subject to university-wide budget cutbacks, while self-supporting programs are free from such restraints.

The University of New Mexico and Northern Illinois University both operate according to such a plan, drawing the majority of their income from their universities' regular budgets. However, the trend has been for universities to remove the athletic departments from their lists of benefactors because of the great expense. This removal has been mandatory in some cases, because several boards of regents have barred the use of public funds for athletic departments. These funds, the regents have said, should come from other sources because of the great expense they add to the

taxpayers' already steep burden. This removal has occurred at such big-time programs as those at Michigan
State University, the Universities of Alabama, Mississippi, Illinois, Texas, and California at Los Angeles.

The other benefactors they refer to, of course, are
gate receipts and outside contributions. Thus, once
the athletic department ceases to draw a large portion
of its income from the university budget, it is faced
with the following alternative; to begin hustling enough
money to make it on its own, or give up its big-time
program and return to a smaller but more sensible one.
Sadly, the great American dream an the Horatio Alger
syndrome force most programs to take the first choice
and try to support themselves and grow bigger. As a
result, the importance of gate receipts and all other
possible forms of income to athletic departments can
be easily understood.

Such a situation is similar to that faced by any
business: produce a saleable product, publicize and
market it, or get out of business.

Other than gate receipts which have been described, the most popular of these forms has been to
cash in on student activity fees to help defray expenses. Student activity fees are collected from the
students when they register for classes to cover their
admission to university events, including athletic
games. Some universities call them sports fees and
others label them athletic or activity fees, but regardless of the tag, their single largest benefactor is
usually the school's athletic department. When a student pays this fee, as mentioned, he assumes he is to
receive an activity pass which will allow him to attend
all campus activities, including athletic events, free of

cost. Often that assumption is wrong. Possessing an activity card doesn't always assure a student of this privilege. Some universities, a few in the Big Ten for example (the Universities of Illinois and Iowa, and Ohio State), used to charge student activity cardholders an additional amount for home-game tickets. Other universities still continue this practice. In reality, they are charging the students more than once to support the schools' athletic programs. A further irony of this situation, which probably should be called the activity pass game, is that even then only a portion of the students usually have an opportunity to buy a game ticket. For instance, if a football stadium seats fifty thousand and there were twenty-five thousand students in school, only half of them would have the opportunity to see each game because only twelve thousand seats would be reserved for them to buy at a slightly reduced student rate. The remaining thirty-eight thousand seats would be sold to anybody who would pay top dollar (usually $6.00 to $12.00 per seat for football).

If the same university's basketball arena seats eight thousand or less, as so many do, the problem becomes even worse; only five thousand students out of the total student population would be permitted the opportunity to purchase seats. At schools that operate like this, the students, who pay the majority of the athletic department's bills, are left out in the cold when it comes time to see the games.

Due to student pressure, most schools have abandoned this double charge policy. But student activity fees still remain a major source of income for collegiate athletics. In most schools they account for from 25 to 75 percent of the income for athletics. Continuance of this support is not guaranteed, however. Recently student pressure has resulted because the students are tired of being the financial fall-guys. They began to check on where their activity fee money was spent, and in most cases, after finding out, they disagreed with the large sums allocated to inter-collegiate athletics. In rebuttal, a few years ago at San Jose State and Colorado State Universities, the students even voted to withhold their funds from athletics for a time. They said the money could be better utilized in other areas more consistent with their interests. Students at the University of Kansas followed suit recently and voted to withhold their activity fee money from athletics for the 1971-72 school year. As the students expected, the athletic establishment at KU refused to give up easily and they fought back. The athletic department raised the cost of student season tickets from $5 to $18 for football games and a like amount for basketball. Previously, students at Kansas had played the activity fee game and had paid double to support sports: with an activity fee which had annually plopped about $200,000 into the athletic department coffers and a charge for game tickets. So paying for game tickets wasn't anything new for them but paying triple the normal student ticket price was a different story.

The athletic department at San Diego State University, formerly California State University at San Diego, has had difficulty lately securing student money too. After threatening to drastically cut their allotment to athletics, the Associated Student Board, the student association that controls activity money usage at the San Diego school, finally allocated enough money to help defray the cost of the college's athletic budget of just under $1 million. Getting the students to allocate these funds wasn't an easy task though. After the students decided to cut their previous year's allotment to athletics, eleventh-hour negotiations by the administration pulled off the athletic establishment's coup of the year a few years ago. As a result, the students relented and allocated adequate money to support athletics and even signed a contract guaranteeing like funding for the next five years. Even though votes in the past on the athletic funding issue had been close at San Diego State, never before had the students voted against athletics completely. Maybe there is a new day dawning.

The lucky athletic machine won the first round for San Diego State, but predicting a similar victory after five years would be about as risky as drawing to an inside straight!

Innovative students have arrived at yet another method of showing their dislike for allotting the greater portion of their activity money to athletics. Instead of just withholding the payment to the athletic department, like at San Diego and Kansas, they just don't pay the fees at all! There is no formal agreement to withdraw funds from athletics, students simply don't pay the fee at registration time even though the athletic departments have planned their budgets assuming the funds would be forthcoming.

This measure is a bit more drastic than simply cutting back on activity fees for athletics, but the effect has been the same—unbalanced athletic budgets.

The students aren't the only ones threatening to remove student activity fees from athletic department coffers, however. The board of regents for Illinois state universities are considering the same. They're contemplating barring the use of such funds to provide support for two of its larger universities' programs. In particular, at Northern Illinois University and Illinois State University, they're considering barring its use for athletic scholarships. The two schools in question each receive about $500,000 a year in student fee money to support athletics—about one-half of which goes toward full rides. Although a final decision has not yet been issued at this writing, if it goes against athletics and the fees are taken away, these schools' athletic departments are going to be faced with the typical dilemma—to continue going big time or not. They will either have to give up their dreams of going big time because they can no longer pay for talent, or keep their dreams and begin paying for it through gate receipt revenue, alumni contributions, and the like. If they take the gate receipt route, they'll be casting themselves into a do-or-die situation; that is: win games, draw big crowds, and survive; or fail to draw crowds and perish. For the most part, all of today's collegiate biggies have taken the same gamble and won. But, there are several who've lost too, such as the University of California at Santa Barbara and the University of Buffalo, who were forced to give up entire parts of their athletic programs because of financial woes, the schools' football programs, in the case of these schools.

Because of the uncertainty of gate receipts and student activity fees, athletic departments have been forced to scramble around and locate still other ways of paying their bills. One of the ways they've found is to establish booster clubs and foundations for raising money; the first for local businessmen and fans and the second for distant alumni of means. Hired promoters and money raisers have made many of these flourish, others however, only limp along.

The lesser known of these organizations, the university foundations, have traditionally played a bigger part in financing athletics than booster clubs. Their purpose isn't raising money only for athletics though; they also raise it for other university projects like new buildings, books for the library, and grant-in-aid scholarships for students other than athletes. But their most frequent benefactors are the schools' athletic departments. For example, the athletic association at the University of Illinois whose yearly budget exceeds $2 million, often leans heavily on the foundation for financial help. Money from the foundation pays for the thirty football scholarships the Big Ten allows them to award each year. This way tax money isn't used to finance the free riders' educations. Supposedly, then the taxpayers don't have a gripe. The football program needs all the help like this it can get because the university's entire fifteen-sport program depends on the football program to recruit good players, win games, and draw at the gate, so it can pay the bills for the whole department. If the foundation doesn't help the cause by paying for good football players, the whole athletic program may go down the tubes.

The University of Illinois isn't the only school that needs and receives foundation grants. A spokesman for the University of Miami in Florida announced recently that a millionairess gave his athletic foundation $1 million. Moreover, she specified that the money be used for football scholarships. The foundation reported that it planned on banking the money and still be able to buy $55,000 worth of free rides each year off the interest alone.

Regardless of whether a university has a foundation or not, every major college sports program today has an organized group of interested citizenry, alumni, and businessmen who band together to form an athletic booster club. Athletic directors and coaches think the main function of these groups is to raise money. The boosters themselves, however, think their main function is to lend moral support first and some financial support secondly. Subconscioulsy, they have other purposes too. Generally, these clubs amount to a group of joiners who gain vicarious prestige through identifying with a big-time sports program. If you doubt that, check them out the next time you venture to a college football or basketball game. They're the affluent-looking guys whose reserved seats are on the 50-yard line or at midcourt, who wear the gaudy blazers and carry the school colors, who refer to the coach by his first name, and who take joy in relating the details of their last intimate conversation with the team's superstar.

Over the years these groups have probably influenced intercollegiate athletic policy and spending more than any other group outside the school's general and athletic administration. Ironically, the amount of money the booster clubs contribute toward the total program is minimal. In most cases it doesn't even amount to 10 percent of the total athletic budget. There are some exceptions, though. The Gator Football Boosters, Inc. at the University of Florida is one. A few years ago they raised a total of $225,000 to contribute toward athletic scholarships. Another exception has been the Golden Bear Booster Club of the University of California at Berkeley. Recently they raised a sum similar to that of the Florida group. These figures only represent one year's collection, repeating with similar amounts each year is not a common occurrence at most schools.

There is a bug in these funds, though. They are usually earmarked for a particular sport (the school's most popular one) and for a particular purpose within that sport, such as scholarships or recruiting. With the exception of a few sports then, the total program doesn't benefit. To combat this, some schools have allowed their coaches to organize separate booster clubs for each sport. And, as you may suspect, that amounts to a real mess by promoting competition between the various sports and their coaches for the public's financial support.

Booster clubs are bigger issues in some parts of the country than others, but in Washington State these booster funds used to take on added importance. Until this year, gate receipt money could not be used for athletic scholarships in the state, so the athletic departments were forced to raise scholarship money elsewhere. Their best source was the booster clubs, and other similarly interested parties. So the coaches not only had to recruit prospective athletes with extra vigor but rich boosters as well.

And just think, all this hustling was done in the name of education. But the beat goes on—win or perish.

About the time athletic directors think they've tapped all available revenue sources for intercollegiate athletics, some eager director comes up with a new source. The latest of these has been the rental of university stadiums to professional teams. The University of California at Berkeley leads the class in this department. They recently agreed to allow the Oakland Raiders of the National Football League to rent their seventy-seven thousand seat Memorial Stadium for a mere $30,000 guarantee, a percentage of the ticket sales over $400,000, plus all the revenue from concession sales. In 1972, '73, and '74, the Raiders will only be allowed to use the stadium for two games per season. That, my friends, is a tidy package, regardless of the game limit. No doubt it will help balance Cal's athletic budget. Tulane has done likewise; they have a similar financial arrangement with the New Orleans Saints of the NFL.

Yale recently followed this trend. They approved rental of their seventy-two thousand seat stadium to the New York Giants. Even though the details of the arrangement were not revealed, the revenue to be received by the University will no doubt be substantial and their athletic program should profit proportionally.

The Big Ten Conference isn't as liberal in this regard as Cal and Tulane. According to conference policy, Big Ten schools can only rent their stadiums to professional teams for exhibition games, which, by the way, bring in some big money; often as much as $200,000 for a single game. As a result of this policy, the huge football stadiums in the Big Ten sit empty and unused all year except for five or six home ball games. To Northwestern University it seemed logical that renting their stadium to the NFL's Chicago Bears would have been mutually advantageous to both groups and as a result, they signed an agreement to do so. However, the Big Ten nixed their plans and prohibited the contract.

In Chicago recently, there was an odd twist to the big stadium rental game. In trying to gain support for the new stadium planned for Chicago's lake front, Mayor Daley said the stadium would make the Chicago Circle Campus of the University of Illinois "the best football team in this country," because of the revenue they could generate from large crowds in the stadium. The Chicago Circle's present football program is strictly small time. Completely supported by student activity fees, it serves the real needs and desires of the school's students. When the school's athletic director heard of his Honor's plans, he said the Chicago Circle Campus had no intention of developing the type of big-time football program he had described. Mayor Daley made a classic retort. "If that's the way their athletic director feels, get rid of the athletic director; we'll put Jack Reilly [the mayor's director of special events and well known for his gala public programs] in charge and we'll have a great football program there. We'll have thousands of people at their games." It appears that the mayor overlooked a few important points. First, the Chicago Campus team would have to be big time and successful first before they could draw large crowds. Crowds follow big teams that win, not small, unsuccessful ones that want to be big and win. Second, and of even greater importance to the future of healthy athletics, the mayor seemed to overlook the fact that Chicago Circle's students, faculty, and administration may not want to be a big-time sport power.

That's not the end of the income game for intercollegiate athletics, though. Radio and TV rights compose yet another source of income for athletic departments. In fact, radio and TV rights are the bonuses that often bring athletic programs out of the debit column and into the black. The problem is that TV revenues are inconsistent because not even the real biggies appear on national or regional TV every year.

At UCLA, football telecast revenues amounted to $257,000 in 1970-71, and the rights for basketball brought in $70,000 during the same year. And the projected radio and TV revenues for football and basketball for the following year were increased to $416,000. Without these bonuses, UCLA's program would have run in the red. Southeastern Conference schools have profited from these funds too. A nationally televised game between Georgia and Tennessee recently brought in over $350,000 to the conference's coffers. And a regionally televised game between Georgia and Florida brought in a sum just slightly less than $275,000. Not only the teams playing the TV game reap the profits, though. In the SEC, the pot is divided thirteen ways. The conference office gets one share, each participating school gets two shares and the remaining nine shares go to the other nine conference schools.

Nothing in life is for sure, though, and TV bonuses may not always be such a bed of roses for the athletic machine. College football may be guilty of a roughing-the-ratings penalty and suffer a loss of 15 yards and possession of the ball when negotiations for the next few years' TV football contracts roll around. An ABC vice president declared recently that "the NCAA [National Collegiate Athletic Association] will have to lower its price demand or become more lenient in the selection of games to be televised." The network says it has suffered losses in the past on the football contract and doesn't intend for it to happen again.

That's not the end to the potential problems concerning TV rights. Citizens of Oklahoma filed a temporary injunction against the NCAA to force them to allow a 1971 Texas vs. Oklahoma football game to be televised in Austin and Dallas, where it was being played, but blacked out in Oklahoma. The NCAA refused to televise in Oklahoma because they thought it would interfere with other college games being played within a 400-mile radius of the area. The outcome was still in doubt at this writing, but the fact that situations like this could pop the bubble of TV rights is not in doubt.

Obviously, revenue from a national or regional telecast would be a blessing to any large intercollegiate athletic program but inconsistent income like this can cause fiscal uncertainty too. For instance, if a basketball team reaches the NCAA play-offs and the games are broadcast, each participating school receives a portion of the revenue from the telecast rights. These funds usually are not expected or budgeted, and a problem can arise for the school in determining how to distribute the funds among their various sports. A similar problem arises when funds are allotted to schools as their conference's share of unexpected bowl game gate receipts.

Most athletic directors dream of problems like this, however. In several post-season events, such as the Rose Bowl, in which Pacific Eight Athletic Conference and Big Ten Conference teams annually compete, this additional income is no illusion. These schools can count on a rather definite amount of revenue from the bowl. Quite often each school receives as much as $150,000 each year from the Rose Bowl.

Recent football successes by Big Eight Conference schools have allowed them to expect bowl game receipts too. Under Big Eight split-the-pot arrangements, all member schools profit when a conference team goes bowling. However, since one of the Big Eight's members, the University of Oklahoma, has been barred from post-season games for two years, as well as from TV appearances during that time, member schools have recently been forced to cut their projected budgets. Oklahoma's excellent 1973 football team (10-0-1) would have received a bowl bid under normal circumstances, but since they couldn't, everybody felt the pinch. Iowa State estimates Oklahoma's suspension may have cost them $200,000 in expected income.

The University of Georgia has shown a profit in its athletic program the last several years and attributes its success to the bonuses received from bowl appearance revenues, similar to those of the Rose Bowl. For a recent trip to the Sugar Bowl, the Bulldogs drew over $110,000, although they incurred a net loss of $12,000 after they paid their bowl travel and vacation expenses. They're high livers.

The Southeastern Conference has an equal distribution rule for bowl receipts, as they do for regular season TV games. NCAA policy assures that the bowl promoter receives 25 percent of the bowl revenue off the top, and then the two participating teams split the remainder. The SEC allows a participating school to keep a maximum of $125,000 and the rest of the pot is split between the conference's office and the other conference schools. Most other big conferences have a split-the-pot arrangement also.

Nothing is for sure in regard to continued bowl game income either, as with televised games.

Post-season game income may be in jeopardy. The University of California at Berkeley and its athletic bureaucracy, the Golden Bear Athletic Foundation, challenged in court the legality of a probation placed on them by the NCAA which prohibits their winning championships or competing in any post-season contests. The foundation said that Cal's fiscal solvency was partly based upon their participation in intercollegiate championship competition and post-season tournaments, and the placing of a restriction against them jeopardized the continuance of their entire athletic program.

The outcome of the Cal dilemma is unknown. But because of this case it cannot be denied that post-season contests and their associated revenues are vital to the shaky world of intercollegiate athletic finance and that a situation like this could jeopardize a good thing. Whenever a major source of income such as this is placed in jeopardy, athletic programs begin to push the panic button. They have reason to do so too, because the result of the Cal vs. NCAA case may alter the makeup and even the continuance of post-season competition.

The final sources of income of any consequence to big-time athletics are stadium concessions and program sales. The amount of money program sales generate is relatively meager, often $25,000 or less per year. But the flowery publicity programs sold at games serve as a vital communication link to the public. Just like the Saturday afternoon football telecasts, they paint a candy-coated portrait of a not-always-so-perfect subject. In that sense, they have more financial importance than the income they directly produce. Stadium concessions, on the other

hand, usually generate a little more income than program sales, but their true value is not near that of the
programs.

College Athletic Expenses

The costs of operating athletic programs, particularly on a big-time scale, have increased greatly too. An increase the NCAA estimates to be over a 100 percent jump during the past decade, when in fact, government figures estimate national living costs rose only one-third that amount during the same period. The worst thing about the costs jumping by 100 percent is that income for the average athletic program only increased by 60 percent during the same decade.

Where can the blame for this 100 percent hike be placed? Obviously, several places, but the brunt of it must be placed with intercollegiate athletics' own nemesis, the grant-in-aid athletic scholarship. Not only has its cost doubled recently, which is the important issue in this section, but for the record, it's also been misused, exploited, and misrepresented over the last ten years too. But more about that later.

The average cost for educating an athlete for a year has risen from an estimated $1,000 a year ten years ago to about $2,200 a year today. Some projections even indicate it may increase to as much as $8,000 a year by 1980. And these figures only represent the educational costs for a free ride. When the extras are thrown in—like laundry and spending money—the average four-year cost of the package today climbs to about $12,000 and the projected figure for 1980 jumps to around $32,000. That in itself is no big deal, but when you consider the total price tag for a university that gives out 145 such free rides, the bill amounts to a minimum of about $320,000 a year. All of a sudden, scholarship money becomes a big deal. In most cases, multiplying the number of full deals awarded times the cost of a single one gives only a low estimate of the true cost of the scholarships. The cost usually runs much higher because of the supplementary moneys, some of which is legal according to the NCAA codes and listed on the budgets, but much of which is not, such as money for plane trips home at vacation time and special loans often given to schools' superstars as an added bonus to their scholarships.

More details of the scholarship problem will be discussed further in another section, but for now, the following three examples will illustrate the magnitude of their expense: Michigan State University spends approximately $500,000 a year for grant-in-aid full rides; UCLA's estimated expenditures for the same runs just slightly higher; and Georgia Tech's scholarship bill runs higher yet, approximately $600,000. Most other big-time schools spend similar amounts.

Scholarships are not the only culprit of the overspend program in big-time athletics. Equipment expenses too have jumped drastically the past several years—often as much as two or three times their previous cost. For example, the cost of shoulder pads for one of the big southern football powers rose from $16,000 to $33,000 in just ten years. The same school's training room expenses purportedly doubled over the same period. Ohio State University finds itself in a similar position. Their estimated equipment costs hover around $50,000 a year, as do their training table expenses. And both these figures represent large increases in the Ohio State budget from previous years.

Coaches and other staff members' salaries follow the same upward trend. It is not unusual for a large university to shell out $100,000 to $150,000 a year for such salaries. Villanova University, for example, pays $105,000 in coaches' salaries and they're not even considered big time when compared to the likes of the University of Texas, Nebraska, and Penn. State. Reports indicate these schools and others like them have athletic payrolls exceeding $300,000.

Skyrocketing payroll figures are not hard to understand when you hear that Johnny Majors, the former Iowa State football coach recently signed a five-year, $35,000 annual contract to coach at the University of Pittsburgh, and that Oklahoma State's new football coach will receive $24,000 per year. Other typical salaries for football coaches are: the University of Kentucky—$24,000; Michigan State—$25,000; the University of Miami in Florida—$27,500; and the University of California at Long Beach—$35,000. Of course, these figures do not include the side benefits, such as the typical $5,000 to $20,000 paid coaches for their pre-game and post-game TV shows, the free loan of an automobile, in addition to other sundry items.

The best contemporary example of the effect of such benefits on coaches' income is that of former Long Beach State basketball coach, Jerry Tarkanian, who recently accepted a most lucrative position at the University of Nevada at Las Vegas. His entire contract package included a $45,000 salary (paid by the school), $15,000 for a TV show, $8,000 worth of insurance, clothing, etc. donated by boosters, and a new home offered to Tarkanian at cost. Not bad.

The real irony with the high-paying positions that account for these huge payrolls is not their cost, however. The real problem is that they are usually listed as nonacademic positions and thus carry no academic rank. Even though it sounds like a confession by the sports people that big-time coaches and athletic directors have nothing to do with education, it's really just a convenient excuse for paying coaches more than university professors. By the way, if you pass this last thought on about coaches' high pay, do so with caution because the chairman of the chemistry department may be shocked to discover that the basketball coach makes more money than he does.

That's not the end to college athletic's escalating expenses. Publicity costs have risen too. Traditionally, twenty or so years ago, athletic departments hired the former sports editor of the school's newspaper to be their sports publicity man and assumed it wasn't a very important position. But creating and continually inflating the nebulous bubble of big-time athletics now takes a well-trained team of Madison Avenue advertising men. It's not uncommon for a big

sports program to employ three full-time publicity
people for the job, not to mention their clerical staff.
The salaries for these ad men, their travel, the entertainment and publicity programs they produce, all
done in a big way, of course, costs the athletic department a bundle—often another $100,000 to $150,000 a
year.

At the University of Illinois, for instance, the athletic publicity office employs three full-time publicists,
one full-time secretary, and seven graduate assistants
who work part-time. The office's total yearly budget
amounts to a hefty $125,000.

Inflation has affected the cost of recruiting
athletes too. Contrary to what athletic directors would
like the public to believe, economic inflation hasn't
affected recruiting costs nearly as much as expansion
has. For example, one large midwestern university
spent a total of $10,000 a year on travel, phone calls,
and other recruiting expenses just a few short years
ago. Today, that same school spends $10,000 recruit-
ing in the state of California alone.

Two years ago, University of Florida football
coach Doug Dickey admitted spending over $60,000
a year on recruiting expenses alone. That same year,
Georgia Tech spent an astronomical $86,000 for
recruiting. Remember, these figures often represent
only budgeted recruiting expenses, they don't include
booster club or alumni expenditures which are com-
monly used for recruiting too. And there is no way of
determining what these latter expenses really are
unless some coach opens up his files to the public.
This, of course, a coach will seldom do, even if he
represents a state-supported university.

How do you suppose these amounts compare to

the amounts large industries spend to recruit their junior executives? If your answer is, "very similar," you're correct.

In the midst of all these figures and statistics testifying to the senseless escalation of big-time college athletics, it seems that a fragment of sensible thought has begun to emerge from the big-timers over the past year or so. In a recent statement, a Pacific Eight Conference athletic director rationalized skyrocketing athletic expenses by saying, "we're 'keeping up with the Joneses.' If our major opponent hires a new assistant football coach, we try to match them. If our major opponent has more football scholarships than we have, we try to catch up. If our major opponent has an athletic dormitory, we get out the hammer and nails. If our major opponent shops for artificial turf, we start organizing a fund-raising campaign. This goes on and on. If we don't work through the NCAA for a solution to limitations, many of our coaches will be selling insurance within five years."

Frank Broyles, Arkansas's successful football coach, expressed a similar thought when he said, "football is in competition for the entertainment dollar and [a team] has to put on a good performance if they want to get their share." And Cal's athletic director, Paul Brechler, said, "we've tried to outdo each other. Now we're caught in a situation where if we didn't try to improve, we'd be worse off financially. The way things are now, you have to win 90 percent of your games just to make the public think you're successful." The athletic director at the University of Michigan possibly stated it clearer than anyone when he said, "My job is poorly described by the term Athletic Director, what I am is a sports promoter.

Either I promote our sports program solidly into the black or I am out of a job."

That is honesty. The athletic hierarchy seems to be starting to call things the way they are. If they're in the entertainment business to make money, then all we ask is that they say so and don't continue to run their programs under the umbrella of education.

Honesty isn't enough, however; expenses must be cut. Penn State's young, education-minded football coach, Joe Paterno, said that athletic budgets could be cut by as much as 25 percent if athletic directors were not such poor administrators, and if they would say "no" to greedy coaches who are interested only in winning and empire building, rather than educating college students. Hats off to Joe. Maybe winning to make money isn't the ultimate purpose of football after all, at least to Joe Paterno.

This writer and several other critics of big-time athletics, such as Jack Scott, athletic director at Oberlin College (Ohio), disagree with Paterno's suggested reforms. They think that maintaining the present system as it now exists, only trimming the budgets a bit, and imitating small college athletics isn't a satisfactory solution to collegiate athletics' real problems. Their argument is testified to by the fact that many small college programs have the same problems as the biggies but on a smaller scale. They recruit, grant free rides, depend on gate receipts, and have a hard time balancing their budgets, and generally do as their big brothers do.

In a recently published survey of methods for financing small college athletics, it was disclosed that the average budget, minus coaches' salaries, for the 248 small colleges studied was $59,513. On an average, 58 percent of their athletic income came from student activity fees. The remaining income came from gate receipts, alumni funds, concessions, state appropriations, and booster clubs. And their expenses have all climbed greatly too. Sounds familiar doesn't it?

So, for the most part, using small college athletics as a model for reforming big-time university athletics isn't the answer. Sad as it is, small colleges look to the big universities for direction.

So, for the time being, big-time athletics face the crossroads all alone, and with little direction. They can take one route and continue toward financial oblivion as they are now, or they can take the other route and remodel for survival. If the second choice is taken, the remodeling program required will not be easy. It will take strong leadership, total commitment, and complete dedication toward renewal and financial restriction. A plan for such a renewal is presented in the last chapter of this book.

Recruiting and Scholarships

The central problem around which all others seem to rotate in intercollegiate athletics is a combination of the troubles associated with recruitment and scholarships, with recruitment more toward the center of the problem than scholarships.

The twisted tale of the relationship between scholarships and recruiting is a sad one, a little like the story often told about the nice kid from a good family who became a juvenile delinquent after making friends with a hoodlum from across the tracks— scholarships being the good kid and recruitment the hood. The moral of the story is that athletic scholarships themselves have caused little trouble and aren't innately bad. In fact, when employed intelligently and with moderation, they are comparatively pure. Particularly if their ultimate purpose is to help needy youngsters, who happen to possess talent, acquire a college education. The same purity cannot be ascribed to athletic recruitment, however.

The misuse of athletic recruiting and its ramifications have permanently tainted the purity of collegiate sports and the once respectable grant-in-aid scholarship. As a result, unethical recruitment must take the brunt of the blame for current problems of big-time collegiate athletics. In addition, recurrent violations of the NCAA recruiting codes have resulted in the renaming of athletic scholarships, free rides, complete with all the connotations that go with that dubious title. Recruitment must also accept the responsibility for the coining of the phrase, "the recruiting game" and the label assigned to it by a Los Angeles sports writer in his story about Stanford's growth to the big time, who said, "When Stanford University authorities decided to go all out for the big-time athletic machine it meant that head coach Ralston had to go into 'the recruiting pit.'"

Recruiting

Why is all the blame placed on recruiting? What is meant by the recruiting game or the recruiting pit? What really happens when an athlete is recruited? Let's take a look.

As any conscientious father of a school boy star who's been recruited would testify, athletic salesmen (recruiters) virtually crawl out of the woodwork in pursuit of high school and junior college sports talent. They spend money freely, speak of the candied world of intercollegiate athletics, and exhibit insufferable gall and perseverance in attempting to get kids to sign on the dotted line.

It wasn't unusual, one father lamented, for his son to receive fifty phone calls or more a week concerning his college choice from schools interested in securing his athletic talents. On top of that, the same boy received countless inquiries, with questionnaires included, asking about everything from his middle name to the type of girls he liked. And those only represented the preliminary recruiting contacts. A well-known eastern university, in addition to all this, allegedly mails enough recruiting inquiry, contact, and sales letters to require employment of two dozen full-time typing and mailing clerks.

But the clerks are not the mainstays of the recruiting troops. The majority of a school's recruiting corps is made up of assistant coaches. However, professional recruiters—usually young, energetic, all-American-boy types who are former athletes and coaches—are also specifically hired by the athletic departments to recruit. Regional alumni and other friends of the university play the role of recruiter at times too. At some schools in fact, the only requirements for becoming a recruiter is the ability to get close to a prospect, to shoot a line of "bull," and to close the deal and enroll the player in school. As a result, high school coaches, church leaders, school counselors, close friends, and any other type of person imaginable have all been employed by athletic departments at one time or another to recruit school boy athletes.

Recruitment of High School Talent

The rules of the "recruiting game" or the general procedures for recruiting athletes take several forms, but the following description approximates the method most often employed to recruit high school talent (football players for this example). During the summer and fall months, coaches assemble huge lists of quality high school football players from throughout the country. These lists are gathered from three basic sources: (1) Newspaper write-ups (football staffs typically subscribe to more newspapers than the local public library); (2) Tips from alumni, friends, high school coaches, and others from across the country; and (3) From scouting reports that the school's own staff has compiled.

The lists are then divided into quality categories. The big stars are listed at the top, the average talents next, and the also-rans last. Each player on the list is sent an inquiry letter and a questionnaire, regardless of his original classification.

Those near the top of such lists are usually contacted personally. Personal contacts are initially made by a local "bird dog" who knows or lives close to the athlete. Bird dog is a name given to a local resident who is a quasi-football expert, but more important, a close friend of the university's football program who checks out local talent, usually for little or no fee. Once such a person makes the original entree, professional recruiters assume the job and the recruiting game goes into full force—the persuasion campaign is under way.

The first personal contact with a high school athlete by a professional recruiter is made during or shortly after the player's high school football season. In-season contacts, particularly on the day of games, are not permitted according to NCAA code. Prior to contact by a professional recruiter, however, each quality player on the list is scouted to determine whether he's really worth pursuing.

Once the top choices are made and the second contact has been completed, the chase really begins. It's a chase because a high school star who is one university's top choice is certain to be the top choice of several other schools too. Thus, he will no doubt be the center of an action-packed recruiting battle, disguised under the sham of helping him receive an education.

At this point, the follow-up phone calls, coaches' visits to the recruitee's home, and the athlete's visits to the college campuses begin, not to mention the wholesale bargaining that goes along with all these contacts. Regional recruiting contacts, made in the prospect's hometown, usually include a fancy dinner or two for the athlete and his parents, at the expense of the recruiter of course. Plus as many "fire-side chats" between the recruiter and the prospect and his parents as are necessary to sign him up.

The first one of these big sales pitches usually comes on the occasion of one of the dinner dates. That pitch normally includes a lot of propaganda about the school, its quality education program (of which the recruiter often knows very little and even cares less about), the offer of an athletic scholarship, and an invitation to visit the school's campus. This may all seem legitimate and ethical up to this point and it often is, at least until the recruitee receives competitive offers. As these offers and counter-offers commence, the bargaining becomes heavy and downright illegal, at least according to NCAA rules.

The next step in the "recruiting game" is for the recruitee to make weekend trips to the various college campuses. There the sheep are really thrown to the silver-tongued wolves. If you've ever accepted an invitation from a big land developer to an evening of dinner and so-called low-keyed conversation about potential investments in his land, and have then been hit with a well-planned, high pressure sales routine, including wholesale closure attempts, you have a fair idea of what a young recruitee faces when he visits a college campus and the recruiters begin putting on the pressure.

For instance, preplanned reception (and deception) committees, primed and ready for action when the recruitees arrive, are all part of the campus visits. The technique of inviting groups of recruitees at a time for these weekend visits and having them participate in group propaganda sessions, which was popular a few years ago, has lessened lately. Now most universities employ a more humanistic approach; they bring their prospects onto campus individually so they can con them one at a time. Aside from that, the strategy of their sales techniques hasn't changed much.

Corps of pretty coeds, organized and paid by the athletic department, usually are the first to greet these unsuspecting visitors as they arrive on campus. At Kansas State University they call their coed reception group the "Gibson Girls," named after head football coach Vince Gibson. At Florida, they're called "Gator Getters," after the school's nickname, the Gators. Regardless of their name or school though, their job is to escort the young superstars around campus and convince them that the entire student body is thrilled to the bones that they are considering attending their humble school.

Not all the big timers use this coed technique however. Some schools depend upon their athletes who are currently on scholarship to do the sales job.

The athletes usually accept this responsibility as part of their obligation as a paid employee of the athletic department.

While serving as head football coach at Yale, Johnny Pont employed a similarly deceptive technique. He had the famed Yale Glee Club entertain football recruits during their campus visits. He evidently knew it would be a little difficult to say "no" after hearing the Glee Club sing the "Wiffenpoof Song" and "Old Bulldog."

Fraternity house visits and parties, blind dates, often with maidens of questionable reputations, first-class meals, and top cabin overnight accommodations, are all part of these weekend packages. Several schools, the University of New Mexico and a few Illinois state universities even go a step further. They arrange such weekend visits, for basketball prospects at least, to coincide with home games. This enables the coaches to introduce the visiting recruitees at mid-court during half time—hopefully, in front of a sellout home crowd. How's that for a preplanned ego trip?

Besides all the showmanship included in these visits, there is also a lot of shop talk. The prospects are cornered by one of the coaches sometime during the weekend and given the big pitch, often in the form of a hard sell. The coach's objective is to have the athlete declare his intent to attend that school before he leaves the campus. For the coach knows, once the prospect leaves the campus, the competition will be hot on his trail again.

In a recent statement, Tim McClure, a former All-American tackle from Stanford gave a description of the "recruiting game" as it applied to him. Not so suprisingly, it doesn't vary much from the general pattern described here. He said, "I was an All-American kid, captain of the football team, vice president of the student body, catcher on the baseball team. I even dated the captain of the cheerleader squad. It wasn't long after my final high school game that football recruiters from various universities started dropping by my home, buying me steak dinners, inviting me on all-expense paid trips to their campuses, where they got me dates and invitations to fraternity parties. It was a pretty heady experience for an eighteen-year-old boy.

"But even then, naive as I was, I began to suspect something was wrong. Here were these square shouldered, close-cropped, middle-aged men clad in blue blazers with their university's insignia blazoned on the left-hand pocket, all trying to convince me that the entire athletic department and a sizeable portion of the student body were desperately concerned that I choose their school.

"Anyway, I finally ended up at Stanford, signing in effect what was a four-year contract. I'd play ball and they'd give me room, board, a little spending money, and, oh yes, a college education."

A heady experience—that's the understatement of the year. Employing such a deceptive program to recruit athletes is a king size, preconceived ego trip which is too much for any young school boy to handle intelligently. Worse yet, it's all done in the name of education. Poppycock!

Now back to the general situation surrounding the typical recruitment techniques employed to lure high schoolers. The use of pressure ploys does not diminish once recruitees return from campus visits.

Pressure and influence continue to be exerted in recruits' hometowns too. The recruiters not only work on the athletes, but on the star's dad, his dad's job, his dad's boss, the boy's friends, the boy's high school coach, the boy's pride, and maybe even the boy's mother, depending upon the degree of influence she has upon her son. If all that badgering by the recruiters is not enough to cause him to sign up, they call out their ace in the hole; they have the head coach make a call on the recruitee's home. Some of the nation's big name coaches, with overpowering reputations, are famous for making these eleventh-hour treks to "talk it over" with a young prospect and his parents. How do you suppose you and your eighteen-year-old son would react to the head coach of the past year's national champs dropping by your home and telling you that your son was one of the top prospects in the country, and that he wanted him to play at his school?

In a disclosure concerning such a situation, Bob Newton, a former University of Nebraska football player, recently told how he was recruited. He said, "First (Coach) Devaney got in good with my parents. He went out on the town with them and when they came back my father said to me, 'Son, you're going to Nebraska.'"

Former University of Arkansas place kicker, Bill McClard, experienced a similar reaction when Arkansas' head coach, Frank Broyles, visited his home: "After his first visit," McClard reported, "my little sister told me, 'if you don't go to the University of Arkansas, I will.' He can come in a room and start talking and in ten minutes you're ready to jump out a twelve-story window if he asks you to."

Although there are many variations to recruiting

high school athletes, the basic format always follows the general pattern outlined here. More important, the underlying motivations always remain the same, that is: to win ball games recruit the best athletes at the best prices, regardless of the means employed, and mention education only when necessary; it serves merely as an alibi for operating.

Recruitment of Junior College Talent

Different approaches, all with their own uniqueness and cunning are used to recruit junior college transfers and minority ghetto residents too. The latter is a hot market in big-time athletic recruiting nowadays. For instance, it is rumored that Alabama's football program spent an estimated $100,000 in one year to recruit black athletes alone.

A recent example at UCLA also gives a good indication of the recruiting techniques, or the lack of them, coaches apply when pursuing minority-group talent. James McAllister, a black athlete who had started as a freshman at UCLA, was recently declared ineligible by the NCAA for the 1971—72 year because he had not taken a test required for college entrance on the correct date prior to entering UCLA. McAllister claimed it was not his fault because no one had explained the NCAA rules on recruiting and entrance tests to him. As a result, a Los Angeles newspaper reported that McAllister suffered emotional torment he hoped other young athletes would not have to bear. Reportedly, McAllister was a victim of a fierce recruiting war between cross-town rivals USC and UCLA. Although UCLA won the fierce recruiting tug-of-war and enrolled McAllister, the University was forced to fight a second war, this time against the NCAA.

UCLA eventually lost the war with the NCAA and McAllister was declared ineligible for the 1971 season. Even though the school's integrity may have taken a left to the chin, McAllister suffered the greatest blow and the greatest loss. All because he didn't know the detailed NCAA rules. No recruiter ever bothered to explain them to him. Thus, he was punished and became another victim of the recruiting game.

Although the same could happen to any high school athlete under similar circumstances, such bizarre manipulations seem to be reserved for minority-group athletes. It's almost as if recruiters feel they can take even greater advantage of them—a separate code of misconduct seems to come into the picture.

Isaac Curtis, the former speedy halfback at the University of California at Berkeley, was a victim of a similar situation during the 1971 football season. By some oversight, intentional or otherwise, he didn't take the necessary entrance exams at all. After completing a year at Cal and participating as a track runner during the spring of his freshman year, he made the football team's starting eleven the following fall. Nevertheless, someone questioned the validity of his freshman year's academic average (a little better than "C") and test scores. The NCAA investigated and found that Curtis' and another athlete's test scores, which were intended to indicate their aptitude to earn a 1.6 grade average out of a possible 4.0 which the NCAA requires for eligibility, had not been filed as the NCAA rules dictate. Curtis and his comrade were declared ineligible.

Whose fault was it that Isaac Curtis and company didn't take the entrance tests, or if he did take them,

who failed to file the scores? Possibly the overzealous
Cal recruiters made an oversight to protect scores
that weren't adequate? Regardless, Curtis and his
friend suffered the consequences. Curtis has since
withdrawn from Cal and enrolled at San Diego State
University where he is eligible to play during the 1972
season.

In an example similar to the Curtis and McAllister
cases, a midwestern football coach lined up a top-
notch black player to enroll at his university, even
though the player didn't possess the grades to get into
school or to be eligible. The devious coach evidently
arranged to substitute another student, who happened
to be much brighter than the prospective athlete, to
take the exams necessary to determine eligibility for
the athlete (the same exams that caused McAllister
and Curtis so much grief). Of course, he arranged the
substitute to take the test under the name of the
athlete. The coach and the sub pulled it off and the sub
took the test. But someone who knew of the ploy blew
the whistle. Consequently, neither the athlete nor his
test substitute were allowed to continue in school.
The coach later suffered some deserved incrimina-
tions, but what about the two boys, particularly the
athlete? Was he misled into a crooked deal because
he was an unsuspecting, naive minority-group athlete
or was he devious too? Did his enthusiasm for a college scholarship and a trip out of the ghetto blind him
to the coach's chicanery? Did he deserve such
punishment? Nobody will probably know the real
answer, but both boys suffered regardless and all in
the name of college football.

Recruiting minority-group athletic talent has had
another interesting development of late too. Agents, or

as the high school coaches call them, "leeches," have begun befriending ghetto youngsters with athletic talent promising they will represent them when it comes time to bargain with university athletic recruiters.

The typical pattern for these talent peddlers is to identify a youngster with athletic talent, to become his confidant and friend by spending money on him and time with him, and then, when the time is ripe, to begin contacting university athletic recruiters to sample the interest. Once they receive some nibbles from the coaching staffs, they cease bidding with them and go directly to alumni who have resources and an interest in their alma mater's athletic program. They do this to keep the transactions off the record so as not to jeopardize the athlete's eligibility.

Rumors indicate it is not unusual for such agents to receive from $500 to $1,000 per signed athlete. That only amounts to peanuts, however, compared to the money they hope to make by similarly representing the athlete when he is ready to sign a pro contract.

The deals these leeches attempt to strike for their clients, at least at the collegiate level, are interesting. One unnamed basketball coach on the West Coast recently reported that he had offered the following package deal to the agent for two athletes: $50 per month spending money each, plane tickets home for each whenever they desired, clothing allowances and two cars, not to mention a full NCAA ride for each also.

California schools certainly don't have a monopoly on the cunning manipulation of entrance rules as they affect athletes, particularly those from minority groups. Recently it was disclosed that the high school records of Kerry Jackson, a black freshman quarterback at the University of Oklahoma, had been altered to facilitate his entrance to the university. Supposedly, an Oklahoma assistant coach asked Kerry's high school coach to arrange the grade alteration. The high school coach took the request seriously after he received a threat to burn down his house. He made the change.

Kerry Jackson entered school with the falsified records and played quite successfully on the Oklahoma freshman squad during the 1972 season. When the grade tampering became public knowledge in June 1973 and Kerry was declared ineligible for the next season, he was shocked. Rightfully, the high school coach lost his job (only to have it reinstated later), the Oklahoma assistant coach was fired, and the school placed on probation for two years, but Kerry Jackson suffered more than anyone. He was the victim of over-eager recruiting that manipulated his environment without his knowledge or his consent.

As mentioned, junior college athletes in most cases are more sought after than high school athletes. This is true for several reasons: first, because the junior colleges produce fine athletic talent which has already been proven (like in the minor leagues); second, it's less expensive to pay for two years of an athlete's education, as in the case of a junior college transfer, than for four years as with high school players; and lastly, big-time recruiters from four-year universities farm out certain of their prospects to junior college athletic machines for a year or two. In other words, they recommend to certain athletes that they go to junior college before entering a regular university. In some cases, this is done to allow them to refine their playing abilities, but most often, it is done for them to boost up their grades to meet regular university entrance standards, which, in most cases, require a "C" average for a junior college transfer. Big-time recruiters usually select the junior college for the prospects to attend in these cases and to no one's surprise, they pick the schools at which good grades are comparatively easy to come by and where the quality of athletics is good. Also to no one's surprise, these two factors often go hand in hand, although not always. Such junior colleges as Pearce J.C. (Los Angeles) and Laney College (Oakland) in the West, Joliet J.C. (Illinois) and Southeastern Community College (Burlington, Iowa) in the Midwest, Miami-Dade Junior College (Florida) in the South and Nassau Community College in the East, have athletic reputations that are representative of similar athletic machine-like junior colleges across the country.

Sending prospects to junior college first is not necessarily bad, but it can become so, as is often the case, when the desires, needs, and future of the prospects are not considered above all else in selecting junior colleges for them to attend. This happens most often when the main goal of the junior college apprenticeship is to pump up grades.

Junior college coaches are in on this coercion too, though usually not directly. They are more than happy to cooperate with recruiters who farm out their talent, because they receive first-class players for their teams and because they're always eager to do a favor for a big-time college coach. Such a favor may in time lead to a reciprocal favor for the junior college coach, such as a better coaching job.

To better assure their friendship with the big-time coaches and recruiters and to complete their part of the deal, the junior college coach often promises to see that the players sent to him are registered in the right classes to assure them of receiving adequate grades. Quite probably, a lot of under-the-table grade giving occurs in certain junior colleges to accomplish this purpose. The practice of grade giving is not as prominent as the practice of "soft scheduling," however, which means arranging an athlete's class schedule so he registers only for courses with "friendly" profs who aren't particularly difficult. This way nobody has to ask a prof for a grade; he assumes the responsibility on his own because he's a "friend of athletics."

Whether a big-time university recruiter has set a youngster up in a junior college or not, it will still be difficult to ultimately enroll him in his school. During their years in junior college, athletes get a quick education into the details of the recruiting game and the athletic machine by comparing notes with other athletes in similar positions. Thus, when ultimately recruited by the school that originally sent them to the junior college or by some other big-time school, the recruit goes out after the best financial deal he can get. For such recruitees, the full NCAA ride is considered base pay; they negotiate from there to get the deal they want.

A recruiter for one of the big Midwest football powers said recently that junior college transfers are the hardest to deal with for exactly that reason. He said they want money, clothes, cars, pro contracts, and sometimes even a guaranteed college education. He also said that none of these things could be legally given according to NCAA rules, even though all have been given at one time or other, under the table of course. Fringe benefits like this are usually given by alumni boosters and not by the coaches themselves, however, especially not the head coaches. Regardless of the rules and who does it, the demands of these athletes are met, the Midwest recruiter continued, because it's a matter of pay-the-price or lose the top prospects.

Under-the-table Gifts and other Recruiting Practices

The stories circulated concerning the lavish gifts and unjustified payments to future collegiate stars are probably more fact than fiction. The only reason they are termed stories rather than actual happenings is that the unimportant particulars of each occurrence suffer as their circulation increases. The dates, times, names, and amounts may not be accurate but the fact that they did occur is undeniable. Regardless of what spokesmen for the athletic machine say, under-the-table inducements are very real and a definite part of the recruiting game whether they concern high school, junior college, or minority-group athletes. One junior college football star, for example, said he once asked a recruiter what he could provide him outside of the full NCAA ride. The recruiter reportedly handed him $50 and said, "We'll equal that amount each week." The opportunistic junior college star took the $50, went home and used that offer as bargaining power in searching for an even better deal. He never considered the first school again because their offer couldn't compare with the counter-offers he received in the meantime.

Direct cash payments, as illustrated, are often given as incentive to athletic talent, but since direct payments are difficult to conceal, athlete dealers have been forced to originate new forms. One such form is clothing. Several stories flourish about such gifts. For example, many recruiters guarantee prospective players that local clothiers, who happen to be enthusiastic boosters, will outfit them in a new suit of clothes after each game in which they gain over 100 yards rushing. How about that for an incentive to gain yardage? Similar stories have been told about basketball players who score a certain number of points per game. In other clothes deals, local manufacturers and dealers in men's wear offer to supplement a prized athlete's complete college clothing wardrobe if he enrolls at their alma mater. When such players enroll, they get the wardrobe.

Automobiles have been another shoehorn used by college recruiters. In one story, the hometown sweetheart of a former junior college football star told about her boyfriend arriving home driving a brand new Oldsmobile 442 following his first fall at X University. She said neither the athlete, nor his parents could possibly have afforded to buy or lease the car for him. In fact, she said, money was so tight for the family that they didn't even have a family car. The boyfriend finally told his girl that a car dealer in the university's town, who was a friend of the school's football program, had given it to him to use while he was in school. Some athletes have received a better car deal yet; they've actually been given cars—not just loaned them. Certain schools in the Western Athletic Conference are reputed to rely heavily on automobile enticements too. With some degree of credence, for example, it has been rumored that a basketball star at a large midwestern university, a few years back, was given a car (with his name inscribed on the side), clothing (from a friend, of course), and plenty of spending money, just to get him to enroll and play ball at the school.

Ralph Drollinger, probably the most sought-after high school player during the 1972 season and who recently enrolled at UCLA, said he wishes something could be done about all the illegal recruiting. Drollinger said most schools that tried to recruit him had offered an under-the-table gift, including cars and guaranteed worldwide tours during the summer, among other items. Even though he knows the offers were not actually illegal, because they were offered by boosters rather than by coaches, he feels it isn't right and should be cleaned up.

Another such story has circulated about the ornaments given a quarterback at the University of Miami (Florida). Supposedly, he received a new car and cheap rental of a semi-penthouse apartment in town, in addition to a full NCAA ride. All this just to play football for the university.

Equally amazing are the fables that surround the recruitment contest over UCLA's Lew Alcindor (Kareem Abdul Jabbar), probably the most sought-after high school star ever in the dismal history of athletic recruiting. Every imaginable recruitment strategy was allegedly used to lure "Big Lew."

The report concerning a recent football star at the University of Missouri is even more intriguing. Supposedly, his scholarship did not cost the university a cent. A St. Louis building contractor allegedly carried his full contract (expenses, tuition, etc.) for the four years of his collegiate career, the total tab of which was estimated at $25,000. This figure does not, of course, include all the fringe benefits such as clothing, automobiles and other luxury items—they cost extra. The financing of athletic scholarships like this by alumni is not unusual, it is a rather widely accepted practice among the big-timers.

This particular tale was a bit odd though. When the athlete completed his college days (not necessarily due to graduation) and signed a pro contract with an NFL team, he split his $20,000 bonus with the contractor. This was not necessarily by choice but probably by virtue of their previous arrangement. The contractor, it seemed, had agreed to pay for the player's four-year apprenticeship and the player was to pay from then on. No one knows the actual details of their arrangement, but it appears the contractor had made an investment in a property in the hope he would make a profit from sharing in the player's bonus and future salaries.

Another interesting story is told about a well-known University of Illinois recruiter, who, in the mid-sixties, sought out the home of a talented high school football player in Memphis. He only had time for a few words with the young man when two high-powered scouts from Ole Miss and Alabama knocked on the door. Thinking three was a crowd, the Illinois recruiter excused himself and departed. Wisely, he waited outside in his car rather than leaving. In a short time the two other scouts came out of the house embroiled in an argument which soon erupted into a scuffle and an exchange of blows over hard feelings about who was going to sign the athlete. The Illini recruiter, seeing this, calmly left his car, walked around the brawlers, and into the boy's house. Consequently, he had an uninterrupted, pleasant talk with the athlete and ultimately signed him to play for the University of Illinois.

The sad fact about such stories, even if they are slightly exaggerated and whether they concern junior college or high school recruitees, is that recruiting practices similar to these do exist and that some coaches and athletic programs justify them because they need good players to win, to fill their stadiums, and to make money to pay their bills. For instance, in telling a true story about athletic recruitment, a midwestern university recruiter reported that he recently traveled across his state to culminate a rigorous battle over a top prospect. His school had won the recruiting war for the youthful star but upon talking to him, he learned that the boy had $2,550 worth of debts (for a hot rod and an engagement ring for his girl). The boy told the recruiter that he couldn't leave town until he had cleaned up the bills. After getting permission from the head coach, the recruiter paid the lad's bills and shipped him off to football practice. That recruiter noted later that occurrences such as this were far from uncommon in his line of work.

Similarly, a big-time college basketball player was recruited out of New York to come all the way out to a school in a desert of the Southwest to play ball. He had a full ride, promises for airplane rides home at vacation time, promised use of a car whenever necessary, and verbal assurance of a pro contract. After concluding his four years as a collegiate player, during which he experienced much team and individual success on the hard court, he lamented that few of the recruiting promises had been kept. If the promises would have been kept, they would have amounted to violations of the NCAA code. Nevertheless, one can't help but wonder, is it not a violation of some other code to make such hollow promises?

Policing Violations

Restriction and regulation of recruitment is a big problem, and there are very few simple solutions. Other than the schools and their conferences, the NCAA has previously been the sole regulating organization for recruitment. Mainly, their regulating has been through the NCAA constitution and not through actual investigation, although the NCAA does investigate and penalize reported infringements of their code. Their constitutional restrictions range from limiting the number of visits a recruit can make to a campus and the use of alumni funds for recruiting, to the prohibition of talking to prospects on the day of a game in which they're playing. These rules all make sense but the problem of enforcing them has become astronomical. The NCAA has four men on their payroll whose job it is to do just that, but with over 600 member schools, 140 of which are big-timers, the job is difficult, if not impossible.

Bill Wall, the 1971–72 President of the National Association of Basketball Coaches, and one of big-time athletic recruitings' most prominent opponents, agrees that the NCAA has an enormous job in trying to eliminate recruiting violations. Nevertheless, he feels the job can be done if the NCAA establishes more realistic recruiting guidelines and if the coaches and their associations began regulating themselves. Wall is not just a talker; he puts his words into practice. He claims that his association turned in thirty-five recruiting violation reports to the NCAA during the 1971–72 season alone, which accounted for more than half of the reports the NCAA is currently investigating. The following year a few of the schools reported were reprimanded by the NCAA. Western Kentucky and New Mexico State Universities were both in this category. They had each gained rapid success in basketball, and at the same time had established rather infamous recruiting reputations. Southwestern Louisiana University, which was also charged with NCAA violations that year, recently obtained a federal court order temporarily restricting the NCAA from imposing a penalty. The order was overturned, however, and proceedings were under way at this writing.

The charges against Southwestern were interesting. The NCAA charged that an assistant coach had altered high school transcripts and forged the principal's signature to enroll two of the school's basketball stars, Dwight Lamar and Roy Ebron. That was not all. Altogether, 125 allegations were filed against the school ranging from such things as awarding Lamar $100 bonuses for good games and paying Ebron a $450 per month salary for services rendered.

Wall is realistic enough to know that investigations do not completely solve the problem. First, because it takes an average of nineteen months for the NCAA to complete each investigation and second, because the real big-timers are seldom severely reprimanded when found guilty. And until one of the real big timers is adequately censored for violating such rules, Wall feels, the situation will remain unchanged.

Thus, as Mr. Wall intimates, the big difficulty with regulations has been their practicality, or better yet, their impracticality. Even if adequate penalties are instituted when a violation occurs, it's still virtually impossible to police recruiting and its irregularities because only two parties know the truth about each case, the recruiter and his associates and the recruitees. And neither one usually talks. There are leaks, however. They originate from several sources, such as discontented recruitees and coaching staff members, college dropouts, players whose careers have ended, irate parents of prospects, and, of course, from rumors.

The most prominent recent examples of such leaks and subsequent investigations have been at the University of Illinois. The most prominent of which was their famous "slush fund" scandal during the mid-sixties. Nevertheless, in 1972 they supposedly had a similar but less publicized recruiting scandal.

Allegedly, the slush fund situation developed because the Illinois athletic department had maintained a bank fund account in their coffers to use for miscellaneous recruiting and athletic expenses. The use of the money in this account wasn't listed in the official budget and its existence was kept a secret. Records of its usage were kept secret too. Several coaches in the athletic department supposedly knew of the fund's existence and several used it to give money and gratuities to recruitees, to loan money to stars, to pay for star's plane trips home at vacation time, and for other similar expenses, all of which were illegal according to NCAA bylaws.

Although the fund had secretly existed for several years, when a power struggle developed within the athletic department over the selection of a new athletic director, someone blew the whistle on the slush fund. As a result, Pete Elliott, the football coach at the time, lost his job and several other assignment changes took place also. It was never proven that Elliott had personally used the fund, but because he knew of it, he was censored for his knowledge. Illinois' athletic program is still suffering from the shock.

In 1972 a similar situation developed. A Chicago newspaper reported that certain athletes at the University of Illinois had been given automobiles and other gratuities by the athletic department. At this writing, the complete story by both sides had not yet been completely revealed, but the NCAA was reported to be investigating the situation.

Shortly after the disclosure of the original slush fund deal at Illinois, local newspaper articles rumored the existence of similar funds at other midwestern schools as well. However, most big-timers have an unwritten secret agreement that no brother culprit will expose another, so the alleged illegal acts at other kindred universities remained hush-hush and the rumors died.

Tapping the source of discontented players or those whose college careers have ended will reveal similar modes of NCAA code breaking, each unique. For instance, upon interviewing several such people from the same school, you'd find a pattern of similar infractions which would probably lead to discovery of a slush fund or some other plan for rule breaking. Nevertheless, it's extremely difficult to gather proof unless a disgruntled official involved supplies it, like during the Illinois slush fund incident.

Not all stories gleaned from the sources mentioned result in NCAA disciplinary action, but they do aid one in determining the general attitude a school's athletic program takes toward athletic recruitment.

The next two stories paint a rather clear picture. For instance, one boy told about a coach who hustled him and his buddy off to the big city to see a pro game. Of course, a free trip, fancy meal, and mid-court seats were also part of the deal. Just by chance, of course, one of the coach's former players was on one of the teams and the boys were introduced to him in the locker room after the game. Also by chance, he threw in a little propaganda about the "old alma mater" and his "old coach" during the conversation.

A second former collegian told an interesting story about a coach who had a reputation for being an actor-recruiter. Supposedly, during a call to the home of two brothers in a small southern town, he discovered that the parents were very religious. So, in their presence, and near the end of his sales pitch, he slipped from his chair and kneeled in the center of the room. He then bowed his head and asked the family to join him in prayer for a religious education for the two boys. Although leading someone in prayer was a new thing for him, the parents were overjoyed and the boys consequently signed up to attend the coach's school.

There are other stories, of course, but the purpose here is not to tell them all but to discover a way of cleaning up the recruiting mess that nurtured their origination in the first place. Certainly, there must be several ways of doing that, but the best seems to be a move toward complete honesty. Honesty toward upholding the NCAA codes, respecting the human dignity of the prospects and the schools, and toward the renewal of inner discipline on the part of athletic staffs. People being what they are though, coupled with the pressure to win in big-time athletics, that's a tall order.

For these same reasons, it is not hard to speculate why honesty in college athletics died to begin with. Honesty has worked for some schools, however. George "Chick" Evans, who retired as athletic director at Northern Illinois University in 1969 after 39 years, told his coaching staff that he would personally notify the school's president and the NCAA of any infractions of the NCAA codes his staff committed. He did so once when an injustice occurred, and the university never had another recruiting problem as long as he was the athletic director.

Honesty isn't the entire answer, for even if its virtue were instituted at this stage in the game, assuming all rules and regulations remained the same, it would only temporarily relieve the system's ills. It wouldn't cure them. In the long run, popping the pill of temporary relief would be of little value. A full cure of the entire disease is the only real answer, or as Bill Wall of the Basketball Coaches' Association says, illegal recruiting will continue to be a sickening business.

Athletic Scholarships

A full NCAA scholarship, grant-in-aid, or free ride, by whichever title it's called, amounts to providing money for a student to attend college because he's a good athlete, not because he's a scholar and not because he necessarily needs the financial help. A full ride provides an athlete with free tuition and fees, books, room and board, laundry money, and some spending money. On the average, as mentioned before, this package amounts to about $12,000 over a four-year period.

Because a full ride is not in its true sense an academic scholarship when awarded, it amounts to a school hiring an athlete to play on their team. Thus, under an athletic scholarship contract an athlete becomes a paid entertainer. That isn't necessarily wrong, however, and athletic departments aren't the only ones who award such contracts. Schools also pay drummers and trombonists to entertain in the school band and everybody accepts that as being legitimate.

If the scholarship can lead to a college education for a qualified student who wouldn't otherwise be able to afford one, it does indeed serve a reasonable need. As mentioned earlier, the problem is not with scholarships but with the way they are handled, or mishandled, by the athletic departments and coaches who award them.

How Many Are Awarded?

One of the most prominent problems is the number of scholarships awarded. Until the 1973-74 school year, the NCAA placed no limits on the number of full rides a school could award. As a result, many athletic programs doled out as many as they could raise money for, usually far in excess of the number they really needed. The new NCAA restrictions now limit the number of football grants-in-aid a school may award to 105 totally, of which only 30 may be given to freshmen. Basketball is limited to 18—there are no restrictions on other sports.

Many individual conferences have limited the number of scholarships their members could award for sometime now. For instance, the Big Ten conference limits its member schools to 120 full rides for football over a four-year period. That means there are 30 full rides available for each new class. Big Ten schools and other schools with the same number of scholarships seldom end up with 30 seniors on aid who are still playing, though. For each of the previous three years, the attrition rate is about 20 percent, or six drop-offs per year. This leaves an average of 12 seniors, 18 juniors, and 24 sophomore footballers on aid each year. So in a sense, 120 is a misleading figure.

The Big Eight Conference is one of those that imposed no scholarship limits on its members. Possibly the recent gridiron successes of its members may be a reflection of that freedom. Nevertheless, the NCAA restrictions now affect the Big Eight also.

Scholarship Cut-Offs

Another problem with scholarships arises from the way free rides are removed from athletes prior to their graduation, which may be done for several reasons and by several methods. Although Big Ten restrictions also disallow withdrawing a student's scholarship because he is injured and can't play or because he quits the team, neither their members nor other universities outside the Big Ten like to pay nonplayers, particularly quitters. So they try to eliminate them, or as the coaches say, "the quitters eliminate themselves from the 'aid' lists."

Even though it's against the Big Ten's and other conferences' rules to eliminate these drop-offs, where there's a will there's a way, sadly, in this instance. Coaches always seem to find a way to legitimately eliminate the drop-offs from their list of free riders. For instance, as part of an athlete's scholarship, quite often he may have a job during the off-season to pick up extra pocket money. Difficult jobs like checking for cracks in the swimming pool, shifting piles of sand from one location to another for no rational reason, or maybe even something as sane as sweeping the gymnasium floor, are typical out-of-season jobs for athletes. When a fellow quits the team, and legally should still retain his job and scholarship, some athletic departments initiate a sudden shift in his work responsibility which will cause him to be taken off the swimming pool type job and given a more difficult one, like working the 8 P.M. to 2 A.M. clean-up shift on the weekends in the Student Union. If the former player doesn't like the new job and quits it, he may lose his entire scholarship. Thus, the former player isn't cut from the list but quits on his own, even though in some cases, he doesn't have much choice. Then, if the conference rules permit, that athlete's scholarship is made available to another.

As with the recruiting violations discussed earlier in this chapter, methods of cutting athletes away from their aid, as in the previous example, are surrounded by mystery, misuse and, of course, rumor too. Not so surprisingly, the same inadequate methods employed to investigate recruiting violations are also used to investigate "cut-off" irregularities. Thus, such irregularities are hard to detect. To illustrate, a former basketball coach at an Illinois state university told of the work system he used for his paid players. He arranged for several of the paid players to earn spending money by waiting tables in the university's cafeteria. The trick was that they never really worked—their hours were just penciled in and they received their checks. This operation was the rule but there were few exceptions. When the university's board of regents or the school's athletic conference rules committee met on campus and ate in the cafeteria, the basketball players were in full waiter's uniform and on the job. Although the coach admitted the service was terrible at those dinners, the regents and the rules committee members were none the wiser to the hoax. Either that, or they played the see-no-evil, hear-no-evil, speak-no-evil game quite well. Anyway, detecting the inequities of this job arrangement was difficult because those who knew about it weren't about ready to spoil a good thing. Detecting cut-off irregularities in this situation was difficult also, the coach reported, because of the same reason and because cutoffs were accomplished by actually making the former players wait on tables for their pay instead of just having them penciled in as before. And since very few of them really wanted to work, they would quit.

Cost

Another big problem with athletic scholarships is their cost, as mentioned. Over the past ten years (as mentioned earlier too) scholarship costs have doubled throughout the nation. When you consider schools like Iowa State University and others in the Big Eight who award 45 full rides in football alone each year and 180 totally, the staggering cost of athletic scholarships becomes quite evident.

Iowa State, Nebraska, Oklahoma, and other Big Eight Conference schools aren't the only schools who overdo it in this area. The recently formed Midwest Conference in Illinois and Indiana, which is already undergoing membership reorganization after only two years of existence, was not quite as extravagant as Iowa State and the Big Eight Conference in the number of scholarships they originally allowed, but they were far from restrictive either. The Midwest Conference limited its member schools to 80 football scholarships for four years. Basketball was limited to 20 over the same period and other sports had no limits. The conference announced publicly they would greatly restrict its scholarships. Obviously, the limits placed on football and basketball were not startling. The restriction mentioned must have referred to the last scholarship category of placing no limits on free rides for sports other than football and basketball. But athletic programs eager to grow big cannot be given an inch. Midwest Conference members were shocked to discover Southern Illinois University, which has the strongest minor sports program in the country and was a conference member, awarded a total of 220 free rides, 24 of which were for baseball and another sizeable lot for each of the other minor sports. Competing with them in the minor sports was difficult, unless the other conference schools became equally extravagant. And if they did, the conference would have to throw the word restriction out of their vocabulary.

The very issue of restriction, in fact, threatened the entire Midwest Conference with collapse. That is, until Southern Illinois and Northern Illinois Universities both withdrew, reportedly, so they could offer more scholarships.

In a bit of a twist to the usual story concerning the big free ride giveaway, UCLA only utilizes about 30 full deals a year for their football program, although they claim to have more than that number available. Even then, UCLA spends over $500,000 a year to support their grant-in-aid program for all sports. More consistent with the general trend, one of the athletic powers in the Southwest spends over $750,000 per year for tuition waivers alone (part of a grant-in-aid), and their athletic prestige is not near that of UCLA's.

Admissions Loopholes

Most athletic scholarship winners meet the normal university entrance requirements, but some do not and those who fit into this latter group bring up another problem area related to athletic scholarships. It revolves around that small percentage of students, usually 2 to 8 percent, that most universities allow to enroll even though they fall below the school's normal entrance requirements. Universities claim this loophole allows them to give borderline students a chance, and it does. However, smart coaches have taken advantage of it to slide some of their less astute paid students into the hallowed halls. When a student enters through such a channel, he often enters on academic probation and must secure a worthy grade point average during his first year in school in order to remain. Coaches haven't let this stop them though.

Grade Giving and Its Consequences

Critics of big-time athletics have claimed for years coaches have registered athletes into snap courses where grades were easy to come by, allowing the athletes involved to make the necessary grade-point average to stay in school.

Critics also claim, and with rather reliable information, that coaches have not only registered players into snap courses but have wooed certain college profs into giving grades (as discussed in relation to junior colleges) to their less scholarly but talented stars. In other words, the profs give the grades to athletes to keep them eligible. An example of such was recently disclosed by a former wrestler at UCLA, Peter Lutz. He said he and other Bruin athletes were given special treatment at grade time by certain profs even when they hadn't attended a single class session. Athletes usually call such courses sure things and are often quite happy to enroll in them, but ironically, even though they get passing grades with little effort and infrequent attendance, the athletes don't usually realize such arrangements can lead them down blind academic alleys. They gain college credit and grades to stay eligible but such courses usually have no sequence and as a result, don't lead toward a major in a particular discipline or toward graduation. Worst of all, taking these courses and receiving grades as gifts doesn't foster any learning or character building for the players—which the great American collegiate athletic establishments are supposed to be so famous for.

The best evidence that grade giving or something closely allied to it really occurs, is revealed by the results of a recent survey of pro athletes. It disclosed the fact that over 50 percent of them left school without graduating. Obviously, there are several reasons why these former collegiate players didn't graduate, of which taking snap courses which didn't lead toward a degree is only one, but probably the most important. Another reason for the low percentage of graduates playing pro sports (football and basketball in particular) is that most of the athletes probably slacked off academically during their collegiate seasons and took the minimal amount of academic units allowed to stay eligible. Thus, they fell behind the normal pace set by four-year graduates. Next, if they happened to be a team captain or an All-American selection, they probably spent a lot of time on the banquet circuit during the off-season which kept them away from the books and helped bring on poor grades and failure to graduate. This last point raises another interesting question regarding the athletic machines. There is a paradox in these "banquet specials" that merits mention. Banquet tours force athletes to give up much valuable study time which often results in their failing or doing poorly in classes during that time. The paradox arises in the content of the speeches athletes inevitably deliver and the audiences to whom they speak at such events. Most likely, the audience is composed of high school athletes and the speeches emphasize the need for them to be good students and place their education above all else, even sports.

The fact that most big-time athletes fail to receive an education, much less graduate, is sad, but when you consider the coaches mastermind that to happen, it becomes even sadder. They encourage players to enroll for snap courses knowing full well they lead to educational oblivion, they promote the practice of taking reduced loads during the season, and they encourage their stars to forego studies for whirlwind banquet tours. In regard to this last point, coaches often cart next year's team captain along when they have speaking engagements, regardless of whether the future captain has studying to do or not. Coaches also often accompany their All-Americans when they give speeches too. But don't kid yourself, this comradeship isn't necessarily an indication of friendship, it's a recruiting gimmick. The coach and his paid captain both hustle players at the coach's speeches, and the coach, riding on the shirttails of his All-American's fame, beats the bushes at the players' speeches.

The failure of so many pros to receive college degrees can be accounted for by another factor too. Many of them just didn't have the intelligence. Several probably entered college with below average entrance qualifications and couldn't have graduated if they wanted to. As a result, they were happy to avoid studying any way possible. To them, the snap courses and the banquet circuit offered convenient reasons for not studying.

Government-sponsored assistance programs for students from culturally disadvantaged homes have also created problems for athletes who use such aid as a portion of their free ride.

Admissions requirements for students receiving a scholarship from one of these plans, such as the Economic Opportunity Program (EOP) or Economic Opportunity Grant (EOG), often allow students to enter universities with less than the normal entrance requirements. But, an athlete admitted under an EOP grant, who has an academic grade average lower than that required for athletic eligibility (according to NCAA rules), is not automatically eligible to compete just because he was admitted to school. He must take an academic aptitude test to predict whether his grade point potential is equal to the eligibility requirement, as must any athlete who enters with below average entrance qualifications. That's where the problem lies.

The James McAllister case at UCLA, which was mentioned earlier, was a good example of this situation and the type of problem associated with EOP grant recipients who are also athletes. As a freshman,

McAllister was admitted under EOP rules. He took the appropriate aptitude test in an attempt to project an adequate grade-point average and he scored well above the minimum score necessary. But trouble began for UCLA and McAllister when it was discovered that he had taken the test on the wrong date, and then only in the presence of two other athletes and the tester. Thus, the NCAA ruled him ineligible, even though he had earned a "C" grade average during his freshman year at UCLA.

Nobody knows whether the test date and situation were prearranged, or whether McAllister's score was rigged (it was about 30 percent higher than a score he had previously achieved on the same test), but the fact stands that things like this do occur but are seldom realized. This case only became public because someone blew the whistle.

Someone blew the same whistle on Cal and Isaac Curtis in a similar EOP situation, as described in a previous chapter. Unlike McAllister, Curtis is not shouldering all the blame. Besides declaring Curtis ineligible, the NCAA placed Cal on probation which prohibits them winning any championships and playing in any post-season games. The NCAA charged that Cal's coaches played Curtis knowing that he hadn't taken the required entrance and eligibility tests. As a result, Cal's booster club has sued the NCAA claiming that the prohibition of championships and post-season contests will adversely affect their gate receipts and thus inhibit their athletic program. Because of these two cases concerning EOP entrants, several athletic departments (UCLA, USC, etc.) are silently bowing out of any further use of these grants.

Several solutions have been suggested over the

years to eliminate many of these athletic scholarship problems; awarding full rides on the basis of financial need has been one of them and recently has become a big scholarship issue. The fact that athletic scholarships are awarded irrespective of the recipient's financial need, even though the majority of non-athletic scholarships awarded by universities are done so according to academic achievement and financial need, has created some problems. A recent study at UCLA established that 99 percent of all college scholarships, except the athletic ones, are awarded according to need.

Although not true for other university scholarships, for the athletic ones, the coaches make the decision about who is to receive aid based entirely upon athletic ability. For the other types of scholarships, students apply through the financial aid office and are placed in competition with all other applicants. The recipients are the ones who possess the highest academic average and the greatest financial need. As stated, this is not so with athletic scholarships. A UCLA student financial aid official summed up the method of awarding athletic scholarships at UCLA and most other big-time powers, when he said, "we just keep score for the athletic department. They deposit the money with us (for scholarships) and then they send over a list of people who are to receive aid and the amount of aid they are to receive. We make no judgments as we do in the case of aid to non-athletics. How can we? We have no criteria."

A true but rather unusual example of what can happen to scholarship money handled by athletic departments recently occurred at the University of Montana. One of Montana's vice presidents, its athletic director, the athletic department's business manager, and several coaches were placed under federal indictment for allegedly falsifying student financial aid records and converting an estimated $200,000 worth of student aid funds into the athletic department's coffers. Spokesmen reported that the university received $4.1 million in federal funds over a seven-year period prior to 1970; of which $431,516 was designated for athletic scholarships. Supposedly, only $203,704 actually went for athletic scholarships, while the balance of $227,812 was utilized by the athletic department for other purposes.

Those close to the Montana situation report that the motivation underlying this misappropriation of funds stemmed from some recent budget cuts which greatly affected the athletic department. Nevertheless, this situation clearly illustrates the need to have all scholarship money and its awarding, athletic and otherwise, controlled by a university financial aid office.

To resolve some of these problems and to give the awarding of athletic scholarships a more legitimate base, the NCAA recently proposed a solution. They suggested basing the award of these scholarships upon an athlete's need for financial aid to attend college. They also suggested limiting the number of scholarships awarded for football to 30 per year and those for basketball to 6 per year. (now adopted)

In 1969 the NCAA appointed a special committee to study those suggestions; that same committee made these proposals the following year:

1. The awarding of athletic scholarships should be based upon the financial need of the applicant. *Need* meaning the amount of financial aid a prospect would

require to attend school above the resources his own family could supply.

2. Need should be determined by the NCAA office from a review of an applicant's financial disclosure form.

3. There should be two types of financial aid:

a. *Educational Equivalent Aid.* It would consist of tuition, fees, room and board plus a maximum cash award of $30 per month. Book fees would also be covered but no cash would change hands, athletes would receive a maximum of $180 credit at the university bookstore.

b. *Aid Limitation.* It means that athletes may receive university scholarships other than athletic scholarships, such as EOP grants and jobs, as long as the total amount received isn't in excess of the amount spelled out under the Educational Equivalency section.

4. Football should be limited to 30 scholarships a year and basketball limited to 6 a year. Scholarships not used during a particular year could be carried over and used during future years.

5. Once a scholarship is awarded to a student, that award cannot be replaced even if the student doesn't use it (quits the team, for example).

The NCAA feels the need program would bring athletic scholarships more in line with other school scholarships, more equally distribute athletic talent, make recruiters become more selective and curb the moon-bound costs of intercollegiate athletics. They estimate, for example, that most athletic programs would realize a 30 to 60 percent annual savings in athletic scholarships alone.

The NCAA's intentions are commendable but the

workability of such a program is questionable. About the only thing the proposal has done thus far is to create disagreement among the big and small NCAA members and to raise some serious doubts about the real power of the NCAA. In fact, at the last national NCAA meeting, the need proposal was tabled for another year's study.

The big-time athletic powers are upset about the need proposal. Bear Bryant said, "I think we should add to the number of scholarships, rather than cut them down. We may have to put a limit on overall scholarships, starting on the sports that don't bring in anything—like baseball." He further said that Alabama would consider dropping out of the NCAA if such a plan went into effect. USC's John McKay disagrees with the plan too, because he feels that it is impossible to determine whether a father can pay his kid's way to college because family income is so changeable. Arkansas's Frank Broyles feels similarly. He said, "Let me tell you, this scheme can't work. If it were passed on a national basis you might have major conferences dropping out of the NCAA." Jess Hill, USC's former athletic director, and Texas's football coach, Darrell Royal, have expressed similar thoughts. Royal said that it doesn't make sense for the small NCAA schools, like Valparaiso and Springfield College, to vote on how the big schools run their business. He too, spoke of secession from the NCAA.

Nobody really disagrees with Royal and his comrades' thoughts about the smaller schools regulating the big-timers' business, but their statements do raise some interesting questions concerning the big schools' real purpose for engaging in athletics to begin with. The most prominent of these questions is:

Are the big-time athletic powers ultimately interested in only winning and developing pro athletes, or are they interested in the educational and character-developing aspects of sports? An athletic official at one of the NCAA college division schools, Pomona College in California, made an interesting statement in this regard and may have even answered the question. He said, "I support the 'need' concept because I think that we are, after all, educational institutions and should be dealing with athletics in an educational manner. But I can't speak for a Texas or an Alabama or a USC. Unfortunately their concerns and problems and objectives are different from ours. The big universities are caught between educational experiences they'd like to pursue and a fight with the pros for the entertainment dollar." Amen.

Those who disapprove of the need program, such as some of the big time coaches and their athletic directors (Darrell Royal at Texas, Frank Broyles at Arkansas, among others), often rest their defense upon the fact that it has been tried before and failed. They are correct in one respect—it has been tried before. The Big Ten operated a scholarship need program in the fifties and it eventually folded. An argument against need based upon the Big Ten's failure, however, seems to be a weak one. In reality, the Big Ten ran their need program with relative success and only gave it up because they couldn't compete against the universities from outside the conference who awarded scholarships irrespective of need.

A Big Ten athletic director described their need experiences and gave a brief history of the growth of athletic scholarships in a recent interview. He said the Big Ten conference schools all built big football stadiums shortly after the First World War, which forced them to put great emphasis on winning so they could fill the big arenas. This all took place before there was anything known as athletic aid. The Big Ten schools then began giving football players jobs to entice them to come to their schools and play ball. The job arrangement evolved into the granting of football scholarships, depending upon a player's need for financial help to attend college. The athletic director further reported that athletes then began shopping for the schools with the best jobs and the ones that would offer them the most money. Thus, high pressure recruiting began to develop. In the meantime, schools outside the conference began offering scholarships too, but not based on need. It wasn't long before Big Ten coaches found that they couldn't compete against these schools for the best athletes. So, the need program was cast aside and the Big Ten joined the other schools who were awarding wholesale scholarships based solely on athletic ability.

Another oft-stated example of attempted restriction of athletic spending and aid is the NCAA's ill-fated "sanity code" imposed during the late forties to rigidly regulate the paying of athletes. It was instituted to clean up the slush fund scandals which developed when over-enthusiastic alumni gave cash to players in some underhanded dealings. The sanity code stated that athletes had to work for their expenses and could not receive any more pay or aid than students who weren't athletes. The result was that several conferences, the Southwestern and the Southeastern in particular, didn't like the program and wanted to regulate their own aid programs. So they threatened to withdraw from the then relatively new NCAA. Because of such pressure, in 1951, the NCAA voted an end to the sanity code and maybe even to good sense.

Even though both of these programs ended, they didn't necessarily fail. Instead, pressures resulting from a need to win and from feuding within the hierarchy of the collegiate sports world really caused their demise—not failure. If honesty could have been assured, one or both of the programs would surely still be in effect. Better yet, they probably wouldn't be necessary by now.

The fight over the future of need in particular, and athletic scholarships in general, has just begun. Only time will tell the outcome, but a definite resolution is needed. Some experts doubt whether breaking the NCAA into a third division would work. They say creating a separate division for universities that want no financial or scholarship restrictions placed on them would be like throwing gasoline on a fire. In Chicago recently, the NCAA relented to the pressure and did create a third NCAA division for the big-timers. Regardless of the outcome, experts agree big-timers could not survive on their own if they had taken the other alternative and withdrawn altogether from the NCAA.

Even though action has been taken, the most prominent problem facing intercollegiate athletics— scholarships and the way they are mishandled—has once again been avoided. Thus, the same old problems remain even though they may take on a few new twists. What is needed, as has been mentioned, is a complete overhaul of the current athletic-machine regime, not just a minor reshuffle as occurred in Chicago.

Coaches, Athletes, and the Machine

If big-time collegiate athletics were a person receiving the results from a physical examination, the physician's report might sound something like the following:

Most of the consulting physicians agree that you (big-time athletic machines) suffer many ills; in fact some say your condition is not curable. Generally, the disease from which you suffer is termed the win-at-all-cost fever and its symptoms, as you already know, are an overweight budget, excessive scholarship cysts, pain in the lower recruitment muscles, and torn tie-ups at the coach-athlete joint. And, of course, as anybody knows, they're all very painful, but what they probably don't know, unless they have suffered the disease personally, is that the most severe pain is felt at the coach-athlete joint. That's where the sufferer is most sensitive.

We know that you (the athletic-machine engineers—their coaches) can face the truth about your budget, recruitment and scholarship ailments, but facing the reality of an unhealthy coach-athlete relationship is probably almost too much to handle. Thus, you may find you will deny the fact, or worse yet, maybe refuse to recognize it at all, at first. However, you're soon going to have to face the fact that there is no cure unless the coach-player ailment is rectified.

Oh so true, athletic-machine coaches can ward off almost anything, except accusations that describe their deteriorating relationship with the players. For, you see, coaches have always prided themselves as being "molders of young men" and "developers of character," the "fatherly image" they feel they carry with their players. So when someone accuses them of failing in those duties, they become upset. Some even rant and rave, shouting, "what do they know, they don't coach" or "they're crazy, look at all the great men who've been weaned on college athletics and a good relationship with their coach." However, such arguments are rather shaky. There are several great men who didn't play sports. And of those that did, there isn't any proof that they wouldn't have been great if they hadn't played collegiate sports.

The point is, sports may play an important part in developing the character of young men, and as long as there's a chance that it does, college sports should be set up so the ultimate in that direction can be obtained. And there are several things in that regard that can be done: eliminate the hypocrisy of recruiting and granting free rides; remove the emphasis on winning; remove the need to produce pros; and emphasize meaningful coach-player relationships that enhance an athlete's learning, personality growth, and realization of his athletic potential.

Paradoxically though, as the big-time athletic machine has ground away over the past two- and one-half decades, three negative human relation side effects have resulted due to the deteriorating relationships between coaches and players:

Respect for the individuality of the athletes has been forgotten; the joy of playing has disappeared; and the character developing aspects of sports have become nonexistent at the big-time athletic mills.

One of the major reasons these side effects developed was due to the overemphasis placed on winning by the big-time machine coaches. Coaches began to think that it was no longer enough for them to just play the game; the overblown magic of winning actually became their ultimate goal. No sports reward had any meaning to them it seemed, unless it was attached to a win. Worse yet, they brainwashed their players to believe the poppycock. Big-time college sports all of a sudden became no fun; it became a business whose product was winning. The mighty pressure of winning siphoned the fun out of sports that were originally created to be enjoyable for the player. The coach's sacrifice-everything-to-win attitude not only destroyed the fun of college sports, but denied the players their individuality and removed the character-developing aspect from athletics, but also began creating a new relationship between coaches and players. It began to resemble an employer-employee relationship more than a teacher-student one, as it should have been.

Tim McClure, a tackle on Stanford's 1971 Rose Bowl champion football team summed this thought up

well. He said, "Playing football just wasn't fun anymore, . . . I was just a guy trying to get an education
who'd been misled. You see, I always thought football
was a great game, and that games were supposed to
be for the enjoyment of the athletes involved. It didn't
take me long to discover that at the college level, at
least at those institutions in the 'major college football
team' category, football is not fun at all. It is a business, a very serious business." Gary Shaw, the author
of *Meat on the Hoof,* and a former University of Texas
football player, echoes similar thoughts in his treatise
which criticizes Texas's football program. Too bad for
Tim and Gary, but along with hundreds of others like
them, they succumbed to the glories of the athletic
machine and discovered all too late that they weren't
really its beneficiaries, but rather its raw material.

Other than the overemphasis placed on winning,
what else has caused the relationship between
coaches and their players to deteriorate? Maybe no
one really knows, but everyone involved in the argument has managed to find a convenient scapegoat.
The athletes and the alumni blame the coaches, the
coaches blame the I-don't-care attitude of the
athletes, athletic directors blame the budget, and the
news media blame anybody or anything that's handy.

The players contend, for example, that coaches
will do anything to win, which has resulted in them
becoming autocrats who demand that their players
adhere to unnecessarily strict disciplinarian codes;
that they are racists; and that they are no longer concerned about the individuality or character-developing aspects of their athletes. The athletes aren't too far
wrong either, as can be seen from reviewing the

Oregon State's incidents upon which they base their arguments, such as the following:

Item: football coach, Dee Andros said this about the rules he issues to his teams. "We don't abandon the concepts of training, discipline, team unity, and morale." Even if it doesn't sound democratic he said, he was "not trying to run a democracy but an athletic program."

Item: Texas's Darrell Royal said this recently, "Now you (the interviewer) for example, couldn't play football for me. I like you, you're a nice looking fellow, and you might be a damn good player, but your sideburns go down a full inch below your earlobes and I've got a rule about that: they've got to end where the earlobes do."

Item: University of Washington football player, Mark Wheeler, read this statement from a list of grievances prepared by him and his fellow teammates concerning racial prejudice and the coaching staff, "The racial practices of the coaching staff have forced us to the point where we can no longer tolerate the playing conditions imposed upon us."

The coaches, on the other hand, who blame the lackadaisical attitude of today's youth for these problems, aren't completely wrong either. They base their argument upon beliefs and statements such as these:

Item: Bear Bryant commented concerning the topic, "Kids simply aren't as hungry as they used to be. I am not being critical of the kids, it's the times."

Item: Florida A & M's famous black football coach, Jake Gaither, said, "You're dealing with a new breed of young people today. I began to see it three or four years ago. Kids who didn't have anything better to do than rebel against discipline, rebel against the Establishment, rebel against the status quo. Kids with their hands out, kids who want everything on a silver platter."

The athletic directors and news media people who choose skyrocketing expenses and scholarship ills as their favorite scapegoats, have sound arguments too, as a review of the finances and scholarship sections of this book will clearly illustrate.

Who's correct? What's the answer?

Even if we could answer that latter question and identify what, other than the overemphasis placed on winning, has caused the enjoyment, respect for the individual, the character-developing aspects, and the meaningfulness of coach-athlete relations to disappear from collegiate sports, would we then be able to find a solution to the problem?

Two psychologists from San Jose State, Thomas A. Tutko and Bruce C. Ogilvie, the authors of some recent studies concerning athletics and athletes, illustrate a partial one. Although the findings from their studies do not completely answer these questions, they have raised some interesting thoughts that appear to give direction to a possible solution. They claim that athletes really are changing. For instance, they say, "The cultural revolution has penetrated the last stronghold of the American myth—the locker room. Young athletes, who have scaled new levels of consciousness, now challenge a long-standing article of faith—the belief that competition has intrinsic value. These young athletes go into sports for their own personal aesthetic experience, to enjoy the game, and they no longer accept the authoritarian structure of sports or the great emphasis on winning."

If the psychologists are correct, the arguments of both the athletes and the coaches—that young people are changing—are correct. They are, if we can rely on this psychological report, entering athletics to enjoy and experience the beauty of the game, complete with its built in satisfactions and sorrows, not just to compete and prove themselves a winner or to find a substitute father. If so, then external satisfactions, such as athletic scholarships, big crowds, and the overplayed hip-hurrah associated with entertainment sports, are no longer necessary at the collegiate level and there is logical reason for dismantling the athletic machine.

This information seems to further indicate that big-time college athletics not only need a great change, but a new emphasis. The information also intimates that a change away from athletic scholarships, win-only attitudes, and pregnant budgets is needed. The new emphasis should be toward the employment of collegiate athletics as a vehicle for molding young men's character and personality, as a means of enjoyment, and as a place for encouraging individuality and uniqueness. After all, shouldn't human development and interest be more important than money and winning, particularly in college athletics?

As mentioned, the psychologists' report doesn't solve the problem, it simply indicates a direction—a goal. There are other more specific issues regarding coach-player relations that must be dealt with before a complete answer to the question is possible. One of the most prominent, but least known of these problems, has been the imposed isolation from other university students the athletic machine has forced upon athletes. Coaches have used athletic dormitories, or as the other students call them—jock houses—as one of the main strategies in this isolation battle. For instance, a few years ago Kansas State University constructed a plush million-dollar jock house, complete with spacious rooms, swimming pool, sauna bath, lounges, and sundry recreation equipment, just so their athletes could be housed together in separate quarters.

Bear Bryant's athletic hotel at the University of Alabama is not dissimilar and serves the same purposes. With few exceptions, most other major college athletic powers also have a dorm reserved exclusively for their athletes. As with Kansas State's, these dorms are usually plusher than other campus dorms, and they are nice in that sense. But because they prevent athletes from rooming with nonathletes, they serve as a barrier, or so-called jock strap curtain, between athletes and other students.

Athletic dormitories also allow coaches to maintain a tight reign over their stable of stars. Although this fact may never be stated openly, the indirect reminder of the imposed control and the separationism these dorms represent remains. Coaches rationalize the need for separate athletic dorms by saying that they encourage team unity and togetherness and that they are not used to promote control and separatism. But, how important is unity and togetherness?

Athletic dorms aren't the only ploy in this isolation war, though. Athletes at big-time collegiate powers eat together too. Under the pretense that athletes need a special diet, they are forced to eat at training tables with special food which is different from the ordinary student's menu, even though it may be prepared and served in the same building.

The coaches who advocate training tables aren't up to date. Physiologists and nutritionists over the past few years have destroyed the myth that athletes need a special diet. The only thing they need is a well-balanced one, which they can certainly get at any cafeteria on campus.

The holiness of the pre-game meal has also been tossed out lately. Researchers have found that eating the heretofore mandatory steak dinner four hours before a game, is no better or worse than eating pizza or pancakes two hours before the game. Then, since training tables still exist, it's either because the coaches don't know any better, because they want their teams together as often as possible, or because they aren't about to retreat in the battle for athlete isolation. Take your choice.

These forms of isolationism don't come cheap either. Most athletic machines spend $50,000 a year and more to operate their training tables. And they often double that amount to operate their dormitories. Were you aware that team unity and togetherness was worth that much?

Another separatism ploy is the priority registration time privilege awarded to athletes at several universities. Athletes are allowed to register before the remainder of the student body to assure them of getting the right classes at desirable times. This tradition has existed for several years at most schools and has been another factor accounting for the existence of the jock strap curtain which has strained coach-athlete rapport. Regular students have not always accepted this tactic as readily as the other isolation techniques either, mainly because it has directly affected them. In fact, student bodies have actually begun outwardly combatting preregistration for athletes. For instance, San Diego State University, has a student government who voted to disallow preferential registration for athletes. As expected, the student body rejoiced over the vote outcome and the coaches complained. The coaches argued that preferential registration was mandatory for successful recruiting. What is the need of recruiting athletes, they said, if they are forced to take pot-luck class selection and possibly have to schedule classes during practice times? The students at San Diego didn't relent, however, and the athletes were forced to register with everybody else. Thus, the jock strap curtain opened up a little bit at the San Diego school. Nevertheless, the school's president recently reinstated the pre-registration and closed the curtain.

No single factor contributed as much toward athlete isolationism as did the advent of free ride scholarships for athletes. Because the awarding of these scholarships was based on something other than scholarship, and because they obligated athletes to show allegiance to their coaches, whether it was deserved or not, they probably laid the foundation of a barrier between athletes, their coaches, and other students. By way of testimony to this obligation to the coaches, Loyola of Chicago's successful basketball coach, George Ireland, said, "I tell them (potential recruits), you're an individual. You're different because you're an athlete, and that means you're specially skilled. Unlike the others, you represent your school in public. I expect you to act like you're on a pedestal, be neat and clean, say 'yes sir' and 'no sir' and 'thank you.'" In other words, do as I tell you and you'll be O.K.

There are other forms of athlete-isolationism too, as well as further information to support their existence. At a recent Conference on Sports and Social Deviancy, researchers asserted that athletes may be the deviates on today's college campuses and not the group that captures buildings as is generally assumed. Findings of the conference indicate that athletes are set apart because they identify with the "establishment," preservation of the status quo and conservative politics, when the majority of students identify with the youth culture, humanism, and the new politics. "If the sports guys don't get with it," one sociologist at the meeting indicated, "to the extent that the main body of the student population continues to accept elements of the philosophies, lifestyles, behavior codes, and techniques for social action of the more radical elements of the youth culture, this trend will magnify to create definite acceptability problems for athletes." In other words, there seems to be some personality and behavior differences identified between athletes and counter-culture students.

The conference insinuated that the reasons for these differences develop because athletes submit to authoritative coaches' discipline, compare their performances to that of others, and pursue goals in a winning-is-everything environment, while the counter-culture group believes in individual worth and identity, liberation from others' authority, and avoids competition, particularly when it involves conquering someone to illustrate superiority. An outward sign of these alleged differences seemed to magnify itself during the campus demonstartions at schools like Columbia and Cornell, where the jocks physically and verbally combatted the demonstrators. Obviously, there are other views of these happenings and the differences between athletes, their coaches, and other students. Nevertheless, there appears to be a definite gap and it seems to be widening and serving the cause of further isolating college athletes from other students and alienating them against their coaches.

As indicated, things are changing. A backlash to these forms of separatism has developed among athletes lately, just as the psychologists, Tutko and Ogilvie, discovered through their studies. Athletes have begun rejecting authoritative coaches, restrictive living and eating accommodations, and many of the other anti-individualistic tactics of the athletic machine. This counter-culture has taken several forms, as the following examples illustrate:

Item: A basketball coach at a big-time western university reminded an athlete that he had cut several classes lately and that he probably wouldn't pass unless he began attending his classes regularly.

Backlash: The athlete refused, saying that the coaches' reminder represented an "infringement on his right as a student to skip class."

Item: A football coach at a big-time school demanded that a "paid" player shave his Fu Manchu beard.

Backlash: The coach was forced to rescind his order when the athlete and his supporters said, "Sure, he'll shave, but he'll quit, as will the entire team."

Item: A track coach removed a TV set from the dorm room of four of his athletes, claiming it would affect their studying habits.

Backlash: In support of their teammates' objection to the TV removal, all the athletes dropped off the team and forced the school to cancel the track season.

These are only a few examples of the athlete rebellion. Similar examples appear almost daily in newspapers and magazines and even more appear in the privacy of locker rooms that we'll never hear about. The story is always the same—the coaches demand something and the athletes refuse.

For instance, one such incident that almost passed by unnoticed occurred prior to the 1970 Rose Bowl. The story finally did leak through when Tim McClure told of the unhappiness of the Stanford players over the twenty two-a-day workouts the coach had scheduled during the Christmas vacation prior to the Rose Bowl game. McClure said the players decided to confront John Ralston, their coach, with some demands about changing the situation. But the effort ultimately failed and the athletes relented. Afterwards, one of Stanford's players made an interesting statement. He said, "as long as football players stay lily-white, men like Ralston will continue to coach. And I'm not talking about skin color. When ball players start realizing they don't have to take everything that comes down on them, things are really gonna change."

McClure said that he and his teammates were disgusted with themselves for failing; particularly, when they heard how Ohio State's players (their 1970 Rose Bowl opponents) had succeeded with similar demands. The Ohio State team evidently didn't want a repeat of their 1969 Rose Bowl preparations, which Woody Hayes had run like a military camp. Thus, they rebelled before leaving for the West Coast. They demanded no two-a-days. As expected, Hayes objected but soon gave in because he evidently knew the choice—give in or no Rose Bowl.

Another bug in the athletic machine that has gained prominence of late which is also related to the coach-athlete dilemma, is the growing accusation that big-time college sports factories are only a training ground (minor leagues) for the pros. The original purpose of college sports was to provide an activity outside of the curriculum in which physically skilled college students could compete against similar groups from other universities. It was also intended to provide a diversion from the rigors of academia. However, these lofty goals became nonexistent as today's athletic machines developed. Big-time college athletics' only purpose it seems, has become to prepare players for the pros. One newspaper writer even accused the pros of footing the bill for certain university star players' scholarships. In particular, he implied that one big mid-western football power has as many as six such players on their starting twenty-two whom the pros are backing.

This change of emphasis from collegiate sports' original purposes to becoming mills for developing pros, evolved slowly and unevenly. Its growth never stopped though, because two major forces carefully nurtured it until it reached full maturity. These two forces were big-time college athletics' publicity directors and coaches.

Coaches have contributed to this sabotage by promising futures in professional sports to players as a recruiting enticement. They've used potential pro contracts to shoehorn players into their stables who were otherwise undecided about which school to attend. Big university coaches only did part of the damage though. Small college coaches, with big-time athletic attitudes, must carry part of the burden too. Schools like Grambling College, Morgan State College, and New Mexico State University, each with more than their share of success at placing players into the pro ranks, allegedly have used that success as recruiting bait too. Thus, they have helped to perpetuate the image that collegiate sports are a minor league for the pros.

One former collegiate star said this about his first encounter with the athletic machine and its purpose in this light, "From the minute I arrived on campus for my first pre-season practice as a freshman, I knew that those guys weren't just college students enjoying a game but were men preparing to become pros. And it wasn't long before I was just like them."

As coaches pushed the pro-idea with their players, the college athletic publicity men promoted the idea with the public. In fact, they've done such a good job that a player who, as a collegian breaks every record in the books and isn't drafted by the pros, the public assumes he must not have been any good after all. In other words, sports publicity men have made a college star's real success dependent upon how high he goes in the pro draft, and not upon his accomplishments as a collegian.

This emphasis on developing professionals not only helped to separate coaches and athletes, but it has also served to further separate athletes from other students, not to mention the disservice it has done to the real purposes of intercollegiate athletics. The minute collegians began receiving pay for playing, in a sense, they became pros. And training pros to win games is far different then conducting athletics as a learning device for college students. As a result, the pro emphasis has been one of the factors responsible for the naming of college athletes "jocks"—a title the legitimate college athletes have to live with, even though it was partially created to describe the college pro.

The metamorphosis of college athletics from a co-curricular activity for talented students to that of big-time athletic machines devoted to the production of pro athletes, as mentioned, was by sports publicity agents and by coaches, but it has also been fostered by another factor—overemphasized winning. The overplayed importance of winning, as mentioned throughout this book, has also served as the catalyst for the erosion of coach-athlete relations.

Jack Scott, a professional physical educator-athletic director at Oberlin College in Ohio, and the founder of the Institute for the Study of Sport and Society, a group devoted to exposing collegiate athletic's current problems and suggesting new modes for their operation, has done more than any other person to publicize the absurdity of the overkill aspects of winning in intercollegiate athletics. He is to college sports what Ralph Nader is to consumer protection.

Scott intellectualizes overemphasized winning at all levels of sport—Little League through the pros—and titles it the "Lombardian ethic." He bases his title on Vince Lombardi's famous remark, "winning isn't everything, it's the only thing." The Lombardians, he says, stress authoritative teamwork, overemphasize the competitive aspects of sports (justifying them by saying that they serve as a training for life which is also competitive), place excellence in human performance above all other human qualities, and see their game opponents as the "enemy." Neither Scott nor anybody else, for that matter, denies the fact that such an ethic has led to many great successes, such as high levels of athletic excellence, both individually and team-wise, but all the ethic's payoffs are not necessarily desirable.

Interestingly, Scott says that those who oppose winning per se aren't completely correct either. The rallying point of the opposition group he terms the "counter-culture ethic" and he claims members of the group base their thoughts on the old adage, "It's not whether you win or lose but how you play the game that counts." The implication being that winning isn't the most important factor in sports and maybe one not even worth considering. The advocates of the counter-culture ethic believe teamwork to be important as long as it doesn't impede individuality and creativity. They believe there should be an equal balance between the competitive and cooperative elements of sport. In addition, they appreciate human excellence but only if it can be accomplished without harming others or limiting the person's growth in other areas; and see opponents as the ones who present the challenge but not as an enemy to be destroyed.

Neither ethic offers enough correct answers, it seems. So there is a need for a third ethic constructed from the strong points and achievements of the original two. Scott titles this one the "radical ethic," but maybe just good sense would be an adequate description. Regardless of the title, there is a need for the third ethic and the last chapter of this book is devoted to the creation of such an approach.

So, whether overemphasized winning is given a fancy title or not, it too has led to the destruction of the once healthy relationship between coaches and their players. Although, as indicated, athletic scholarships are the biggest single reason for these strained relations, the overemphasis on winning led to the need for scholarships in the first place.

Racism is another area that has adversely affected the once respected coach-athlete relationship. Minority-group athletes, particularly blacks, have charged big-time coaches with using them and their talent and then reciprocating with little or no respect for their individuality or their race. Two major issues have created this problem: alleged discrimination charges against coaches by minority-group athletes and the pressure exerted by militant minority groups for athletes to join their ranks and support their causes. The latter problem has diminished lately, commensurate with the slackening of firm-stand, minority-group militancy on college campuses which was so prevalent during the late sixties. The charges of discrimination have remained, however, and have already been responsible for the early retirement of many college coaches; who've said, they were "just plain tired of being called a racist."

The basic discrimination problems arose because minority-group athletes interpreted coaches' authoritarianism as discrimination. Whether this interpretation was correct will probably never be known. Nevertheless, the athletic departments throughout the country thought the problem serious enough that many of them stopped recruiting blacks and Chicanos with the hope that the problem would conveniently disappear. Many other big-time athletic powers hired minority-group coaches instead of calling a halt to their recruitment of blacks. Maybe they (the latter group) knew where their bread was buttered.

Although there are several, the best example of the discrimination charges as they relate to coaches and athletes is the situation at the University of Washington. In 1968, Washington's black football players complained that the coaching staff was stacking black players in certain positions to limit the number of black first stringers. They further claimed that the coaches administered harsher discipline to the blacks and interfered in their private lives by criticizing their dating white girls and fraternizing with so-called militant troublemakers. The black athletes demanded a black coach be hired and that the discrimination be ended. After a university committee investigated the situation, it agreed, and the athletic department was forced to meet their demands.

The situation at Washington improved for a time. Then, in 1969, Jim Owens, the football coach, suspended four black players from his team for not showing him a "100 percent loyalty commitment." The blacks rebelled again and as a result, three of the four were reinstated. In addition, another black assistant coach was hired, as was a black assistant athletic director.

To complicate things further, Harry Edwards, the author of *The Revolt of the Black Athlete* and organizer of the 1968 Olympic boycott by blacks, arrived on the University of Washington campus. He urged the black athletes to stand firm and he called the athletic depart-

ment's black staff members "establishment niggers."
As expected, Edward's visit stirred up old issues and
rekindled the discrimination flame.

Washington's racial discrimination problems still
exist today but for the time being they're lying dor-
mant, as are similar racial issues at other universities;
such as San Jose State, Indiana University, Arizona
State, and others. Obviously, the racism problem as
related to collegiate athletics hasn't ended yet; it's
still very much alive at most big-time athletic schools
and it still plagues the relationship between coaches
and athletes. Racism still remains one of collegiate
sport's hush-hush topics. In fact, many university
presidents list it as their number one athletic problem
even above finances.

Generally, the presidents feel racism is a little like
an iceberg; only a small portion of its total is visible.
Their feelings seem to have a basis too; at least one
recent investigation into the racism issues indicates
this to be the case. Robert L. Green, director of the
Center for Urban Affairs at Michigan State University
and Joseph McMillian, director of the Equal Opportunity Programs at the same school, and their associates recently reported the findings of an investigation
they had made into the plight of black athletes in the
Big Ten Athletic Conference. Their study consisted of
an analysis of a questionnaire completed by black
athletes from all member schools. The analysis disclosed that all of the athletes surveyed (100 percent)
felt their coaches expected them to remain
academically eligible, even though only a few of the
athletes (1 percent) felt their coaches expected them
to graduate. To facilitate their continued eligibility, the
athletes reported, their coaches counseled them into

snap courses which were not necessarily part of the curriculum needed for them to graduate. They felt this was done because the coaches had low expectations of their abilities to succeed academically. Such expectations seem not to be without foundation, however. Black athletes seem to live up to their coaches' expectations for they often do poorly scholastically and thus, fail to graduate. In fact, the portion of the Michigan State study that surveyed former athletes six years after completion of their athletic participation, confirmed this. It disclosed the fact that 82.3 percent of the white athletes surveyed had graduated by that time, but only 46.5 percent of the black athletes had done likewise.

After revealing several other similarly dismal statistics, the study concluded by stating that the Big Ten Conference failed to provide an education for the majority of its black athletes and had used them to win games, attract spectators, and draw financial gains.[1]

If the findings of this study are consistent with situations in other athletic conferences, and from my interviews with several prominent officials within such conferences there is every indication that it is, we certainly have not heard the last word yet from the nation's contingency of black athletes. Once information such as this study's results become more widely known, black athletes may begin questioning the true value of utilizing intercollegiate athletics as a vehicle by which to obtain a college degree. The free ride scholarship they now accept in the hope of receiving a

[1] Robert L. Green, et. al. "The Status of Blacks in the Big Ten Athletic Conference: Issues and Concerns," A report to the annual Big Ten Athletic Conference Meeting, March, 1972.

free education, may lose its appeal. If so, we may be witnessing the waning years of the black athletes' dominance of college athletics and a total breakdown in black athlete-coach relationships, particularly in the sports of football and basketball.

Recognizing this trend, and as a result of the Greene study, the Big Ten Conference recently approved a program aimed at helping black athletes obtain degrees. Basically, the program does two things; creates the post of Advisor to the Commissioner for the program and approves the extension of financial aid to a fifth year for all athletes, especially blacks who have not yet graduated.

Although the Big Ten program may help recruit more black athletes and appease the ones now enrolled, it skirts the main issues of the racism problem in big-time athletics. These problems can be solved to a great degree, however, by de-emphasizing the importance of athletic scholarships and the Madison Avenue recruiting techniques that surround them.

Most sociologists agree that America's problems associated with ethnic understanding or the lack of it, did not originate on the college campuses but within the entire sphere of today's society. As a result, it can be assumed that the problem occurs throughout the entire scope of American life and not just in the arena of collegiate athletics; however, athletics have certainly become one of the problem's most prominent showcases. Most probably, such prominence, to a degree anyway, is unavoidable until such time that the absence of ethnic understanding which permeates our total society becomes a less prominent issue. The current chore for athletic people is to lessen the degree to which intercollegiate athletics remain a worthwhile showcase for the problem. If anything, athletics should set an example of ethnic camaraderie and togetherness, not separatism.

This can best be done by lessening the spectacle approach big-time athletic machines now make of collegiate sports: limit the scholarships available and the underhanded, non-caring manner in which athletes are presently recruited and used to serve the machines' goals and not the students'—especially as this relates to American minority-group athletes.

Experience has shown that many people interested in collegiate athletics are unable to accept the aforementioned as a realistic solution to the black athlete problem and the negative effect it is having on universities in general and coach-athlete relationships in particular. Such people argue that the more pressing, immediate problems, such as how to avoid black athlete boycotts and so forth, must be solved first. This viewpoint, however, sidesteps the main issue; black athletes are not the problem, it is the corrupt, misdirected, big-time intercollegiate athletic system, of which black athletes are only a part, which is the real problem.

In retrospect to this section concerning coaches, athletes, and the machine, it appears that the most distressing of all issues facing the athletic machine is not its finances, although they are indeed extravagant and highly publicized, and not its recruiting and scholarship problems, although they are both employed illegally at most athletic mills. But its real problem is its complete neglect of human dignity; particularly, the absence of respect for individuality, the joy of participating, and its avoidance of using athletics as a tool

for developing young men's character. And these
three issues are all indicative of the deteriorating kinship between players and their coaches.
Even if all the other problems with big-time college athletics remained (overblown finances, excessive scholarships, and the like), but the human
relations problems could be eliminated, (in other
words, increased rapport between coaches and players) big-time college athletics could once again exist
as a tool for learning and there would be no need to
dismantle it. However, such is not the case.

Change or Perish

Where does the athletic machine go from here? Does it continue on as it has, only with minor alterations, and hope that its problems melt away? Or, should it alter its course altogether and head down a new path?

If the first choice is selected, one can't help but wonder whether minor alterations in the makeup of big-time college athletics, such as placing limits on the number of scholarships and basing their award upon need, would bring enough change to prevent its pending downfall. If the second choice were taken, and the present machines were completely dismantled and new ones built, the probable outcome would be a mystery. The prime question in that regard is: would the excitement of college sports cease altogether, or would collegiate sports blossom into the thrilling games and competition played by regulation students they were once intended to be?

If anyone knew all the answers and could foretell which solution was best, a book like this, which discusses the rapidly degenerating big-time collegiate scene wouldn't be necessary. But since it is, maybe it can create enough debate concerning the athletic machine and its drawbacks to stimulate serious thought concerning a worthwhile plan for its change. Some people have already given this subject some thought and have suggested some potential solutions. Currently, there seem to be three such solutions that have gained the most prominence and created the most debate.

First of these is the dream that big-time college sports should be returned to their former days of "purity" when they were conducted for students. Inter-school athletics were originally run as clubs for the students, and were completely operated by them too. The students hired their own mentors (usually talented alumni athletes) who served as coach-managers on a seasonal basis; the universities themselves had nothing to do with the clubs or their managers. It wasn't long, however, before the clubs began developing problems. Winning became their main goal and they started recruiting the best players possible and financing their education to accomplish it. As a result, the originally pure sports club programs began to deteriorate due to lack of control. The universities were then forced to step and regulate them. Thus, the early purity of club sports was short-lived.

Nevertheless, just because club sports failed once doesn't mean they couldn't succeed today and present a workable solution to our polluted big-time athletic machines. In fact there are some successful club sports programs presently operating that are very workable. One example is at Loyola University in Los Angeles. At Loyola a football club program has operated successfully for four years. The university itself has had nothing at all to do with the administration or financing of the football club; the student body has footed most of the club's bills by paying a yearly football fee which they assessed themselves. When the students originally approved such a fee, they charged themselves each twenty dollars per year, but two years later, they lowered that to seven dollars per year.

When the football club began in 1967, football had been nonexistent at Loyola for sixteen years. Even though it had been a dead issue since 1951, Loyola wasn't a newcomer to the game; the school had fielded a big-time team in the late twenties and early thirties. So big, in fact, that in 1932 the Loyola "blood and gutters" held a powerful Southern Cal eleven, that year's National Champs and Rose Bowl victors, to a slim 6–0 victory. That was such a glory for Loyola that it is still discussed on the Los Angeles campus. After those years of glory, times grew bleak, good athletes and consistent winning began to cost more, and the Loyola Lions finally gave up their big-time hopes and they soon gave up their football program altogether.

Evidently the football fever didn't die out completely, though, as evidenced by the small group of boys that banded together to rekindle the flame and form a football club. Soon after the group's rebirth, however, the school's administration indicated they were still opposed to football by refusing to recognize the club as part of the school's athletic program or to give it any financial support. Being determined, the club decided to finance its own program. They asked their fellow students for money. By a lopsided margin of 90 percent, the students initially voted in favor of assessing themselves the twenty dollar fee just mentioned.

With this and their own pocket money, the members hired a coach, bought equipment, health insurance, shower soap, towels, tickets, and everything else they needed to run their program. Although the administration had failed to lend financial help or intercollegiate recognition, it didn't completely ignore them; it allowed them to practice and play their games on the old campus field. A club football program was born.

"The biggest problem they faced after four years of operation," according to Jim Brownfield, the club's first coach, "was finding other clubs to play." As a result, they were always playing nonclub teams with subsidized players, comparatively large budgets and fully paid coaching staffs. Most of the schools they played, according to the former coach, talked about giving up their regulation programs and playing on a club basis too, but none of them actually got around to doing it. It was, again according to the coach, as if they were all waiting for the other guy to make the move first. Don't feel too sorry for the coach and his band of club footballers though. To date, they've posted a winning season each year of their existence and against competition which is mostly nonclub. In 1969, they were named the number one club football team in the nation by the National Club Football Association, and affiliate of the NCAA.

Winning doesn't seem to be the ultimate goal at Loyola, however. Other things are important too. Their former coach said it this way, "Our kids play football because they love the game. Nobody ever quits the squad. We had forty-six men report for our first practice and we suited up forty-six men Saturday night (their first home game of the 1972 season)."

If the time ever comes when the students no longer want a club football program at Loyola, they will simply dissolve it and it won't even require an official act of the board of trustees. In fact, the campus is currently debating just such an issue; should they continue to support the football club or allocate their money to other purposes? At this writing the question was unresolved, but regardless of the eventual outcome the students will make the decision because it is their activity, and for club sports, that's the correct road to travel.

That's not the end of the Loyola story. Besides the students' involvement, there are some other beauties of club sports as illustrated by the Loyola example which are significant. Balancing the budget, recruiting, and scholarships seem not to be big problems for club teams like Loyola's. Mainly, because they have no scholarships and because they do no recruiting. That doesn't mean they don't look for good players however. They do recruit on their own campus, in the gym classes, and English classes, and anywhere they can find an eager player.

The budget also benefits because the club doesn't scout their opponents, or take movies of their games—it costs too much, and besides, they're playing the game for fun, not trying to run a profit-making business like the big "athletic mills."

As far as the budget goes, if the students continue to support the club financially, it will probably survive. Meanwhile, the club members hustle on their own for a little extra money to pay their expenses, like bus fare to the next game and new soap for the shower room. Prior to their first home game of 1971, in fact, the team members put on a pot-luck dinner and rally to raise money, which indicates their real dedication to a sport. One cannot help but wonder who cooked the food, maybe the left guard is a gourmet chef too?

In review, then, the Loyola football club is no different than any other campus club, such as the Chess Club or the Debate Club. It's sponsored and operated by the students. The Loyola example, whether it survives or not, seems to be living proof that successful athletic programs don't need to be big, expensive, and inhuman. Loyola is not just an isolated example either. The University of Chicago, Georgetown University in Washington, D.C., and Fordham University (of "Fordham Flash" fame) in New York present other workable examples.

At the University of Chicago, for instance, intercollegiate football and basketball were nonexistent after 1939. A decade or so ago, however, a group of students interested in football formed a club team. They were so eager to play, reports current athletic director Walter Hass, that they even used the equipment left over from 1939. It was not long before they had their own new equipment though and were playing a full schedule—and all for fun. In fact, things went so well for this group and the program seemed so sensible to the university in regard to educational goals and suitable outcomes, that they stepped in, and in 1969, with the full support of the student body, rekindled a twelve-sport university-sponsored and administered intercollegiate sports program.

Athletic Director Hass reports that none of this

would have taken place without the students taking the lead by organizing a club program. They proved that sports don't need to be big and expensive to be worthwhile.

The University of Wisconsin also operates a successful club sports program. Theirs, however, operates as a sister program to the school's big-time intercollegiate setup. Nevertheless, it presents a worthwhile alternative to many Wisconsin students who are interested in participating in sports rather than in just observing them.

These examples definitely illustrate that club sports offer a worthwhile alternative to the muddle of today's big-time athletic machines. Maybe athletic people have learned enough over the last three quarters of a century about athletics to make sports clubs work this time, even though they failed earlier. The trick, it seems, as the Loyola coach said, is for the university administration to impose limits on the club programs and see that they are enforced.

So when collegiate sports critics suggest returning big-time athletics to the former days of athletic purity, if they are referring to the original days of club sports (of which the Loyola and Wisconsin situations are contemporary examples) that's fine. But if they're referring to any of intercollegiate athletic's subsequent former days, they're misinformed about the meaning of purity. Because, it was in those other early days of collegiate sports, shortly after World War I, that universities gave birth to the entire big-time athletic machine mess by building huge football arenas and forcing themselves to draw big crowds to pay off the mortgages. Those were the days when Notre Dame and other big-time powers traveled across the country challenging all comers, spending big money and drawing big gates. Thus, things at that time weren't much different from what exists today.

Those were also the days of the "All-American Boy" type heroes, like Notre Dame's George Gipp. Reflect a minute though—were they really heroes? Were Gipp and other paid stars of yesteryear much different than their counterparts of today? Did you know, for instance, that on two different occasions the gallant Gipper deserted Notre Dame because of better financial offers from other schools; namely, the University of Michigan and the University of Detroit (you see, cheating and illegal recruiting were present then too)? Luckily for the Irish, Knute Rockne was able to drag the Gipper home both times. This same Gipper died of pneumonia after his playing days were finished while he was on a mid-winter spree in Chicago.

An All-American boy indeed! One can't help but wonder, after the early stages of the sports clubs passed if collegiate sports ever had another period of purity and sanity. It seems that the candied tales of college sports' glorious yesteryears are just that— candied tales. Consequently, a return to the early heydays of big-time college athletics, with the exception of the early years of club sports, certainly is not the answer to the athletic machine's dilemma.

The second solution that has made a lot of noise lately, suggests big-time athletics be deflated to the level of small college sports. This could be accomplished, its proponents claim, by doing away with athletic scholarships, placing ceilings on athletic budgets, and cutting back on coaching staffs. The long-lasting effects of such a reform are in doubt, however. All the factors listed could certainly be limited, but removing the sacrifice-everything-to-win attitude of the coaches, whether they be big- or small-timers, would be next to impossible. As long as that attitude exists, it would only be a short time before the big-time cycle would repeat itself. The athletic machine would inevitably develop again and the same old problems would reappear. Most small colleges and universities follow the lead of the big-timers anyway and aren't as free from the ills that plague them as we're led to believe. Most of them long for the day when they too can go big time.

Schools such as Northern Illinois University, the University of Southern Mississippi, and the California State Universities at Long Beach and San Diego State for instance, once operated successful small college athletic programs, not only in the win-loss columns, but by fostering an athlete's total growth through the medium of sports. But ambition got the best of them and they gave way to their lust for greater glories and big-time stature. The schools (with the exception of Long Beach State) have all recently achieved the first step toward their goal; they have been elevated from the College Division to the Major College Division of the NCAA. As a result, they have all rearranged their athletic philosophies and now place great emphasis on winning, drawing big crowds, massive recruiting, and full rides. Unfortunately for them, their success in the big leagues, for the most part, has been anything but glorious. They not only lose regularly on the field to the biggies but their stadiums are half-empty most of the time too.

The four universities mentioned are not exceptions, they are more like the rule. For every section of the country has several colleges or universities (the title is meaningless) whose athletic programs are called small college but whose athletic philosophy and attitude are strictly big time. Other schools in this category are: Westchester State (N.Y.), Slipperyrock State (Pa.), Louisiana Tech., Arkansas State, the University of Minnesota at Duluth, Illinois State, Southern Illinois, Adams State (Col.), and West Texas State, among others. Although not all these schools have received their big-time union card from the NCAA, their athletic philosophies indicate they are striving toward that goal.

In football, a university is not officially listed as an NCAA Major College Division team until 60 percent of its schedule consists of other major college division teams. And that's no easy thing to obtain by the way, simply because big-timers don't want to risk a loss of prestige by playing and possibly losing to a school listed as small college. The only reason some have been lured to do so is money. Some small-timers with big-time aspirations offer large enough guarantees to entice University Division teams to play them. Guarantees from $30,000 to $50,000 are not uncommon in these instances. When they're compared to the $100,000 guarantees the major colleges pay each other for games, they don't seem like much, but remember, the schools offering these $30,000 to $50,000 bonuses are supposed to be small time.

Discussing the difficulties these schools have scheduling major universities is beside the point. The point is that there are several such schools across the country that are flirting with athletic disaster by trying to go big time. Not only can't they compete with the power mills, but they often can't draw big enough crowds to pay for their growth. As a result, they will probably lose most of their games (at least those against the established big-timers), and very possibly their entire program may be forced to fold as a result.

Once this escalation process begins for a college or university with what is identified as a small college athletic status, its athletic budget begins to soar and the demands for winning teams and big gates become greater than ever before. A perfect example is California State at Long Beach. Although they haven't yet received major college ranking from the NCAA, Long Beach desires to be big time and dreams of the day when they'll achieve that dubious award. To bring their longing to reality they've hired coaches who place winning on the top of their priority lists and who are dedicated recruiters. That doesn't solve their problems, however. The coaches have discovered they cannot compete in local recruiting battles with the established biggees, such as their neighbors USC and UCLA; they are forced to go out-of-state to recruit. There they base their success upon selling their beautiful campus and their close proximity to surfing beaches. Recently one of the coaches listed another recruiting plus which Long Beach enjoys. They practice football on the same field as the Los Angeles Rams, so several of the players have become acquainted with the pro players. When they then return to their hometowns and spread the word (the coaches hope), other athletes take note and give Long Beach State a second look.

More active recruiting isn't the only thing that their big-time dreams have created. Long Beach's financial structure is undergoing a change too. They now depend more heavily upon gate receipts, and as a result, better competition to encourage larger crowds. To

supplement the gate receipts (which are meager—
Long Beach's average home football attendance in
1972 was 5,500), a booster club has been formed and
now actively solicits financial resources for the growing program. In 1972 the groups raised $200,000, only
one-half of which was cash, the other being pledges.
Most of this money went toward grants-in-aid. But
meeting everyday operating expenses is tough, so
alumni support has also been organized in the hope of
increasing donations for athletics.

Long Beach needs all the financial help it can get
too, for on the other side of the ledger, expenses are
rising. Guarantees for games have increased by twen-
tyfold, as have coaches' salaries, the costs of intersectional travel, publicity, recruiting expenses and
scholarship outlays. Thus, the $500,000 now used to
pay the bills for football and basketball, which comes
from state appropriations and student activity fees, is
looking rather meager.

Even though Long Beach's program costs more to
operate than before, the pressure to win has become
greater and the training of players for the pros more
prominent, hope for big-time status continues to grow
among Long Beach's coaches and athletic bureaucracy. They base that hope upon some of their program's recent successes, such as: Long Beach State
and Ohio State were the only two schools in 1971 to
have both a football and basketball player chosen in
the first round of the pro-draft; they've defeated San
Diego State in football two years running, even though
San Diego hasn't been ranked nationally and is
another small school striving to go "big"; and their
basketball team reached the NCAA playoffs three
years in succession (1970–72) and was only

narrowly defeated 57–55 by National Champions UCLA in 1971.

Typically, none of Long Beach's success is based upon the number of students who participated or benefited from the sports but only upon winning and developing pro prospects. That in itself presents a rather sad commentary on athletic programs with big-time dreams.

The following statement indicates the unique attitude aspiring athletic programs such as Long Beach's have developed in their quest for greater glory. It is from a newspaper article that appeared concerning the big-time aspirations of another rapidly growing university with similar dreams. It said that the football coach and athletic director at the particular school "can visualize their school's football program on an equal footing with the nation's powers.

"It's simply a matter of getting more scholarships and, perhaps more important, getting their fair share of the top high school athletes being turned out each year." Their unique philosophy is, get more money for more scholarships, better recruiting and bigger programs, and in no time you'll be able to compete with the big-timers.

There are yet other examples of small schools trying to go big. One small East Coast college, for example, whose football budget is a comparatively low $50,000, excluding financial aid, has an athletic philosophy that is anything but small time. The philosophy is directly attributable to the school's coach whose sole aim in life is to produce winning teams and move up the coaching ladder to a big-time college job and eventually to the pros. He is willing to sacrifice almost everything else for winning. To this coach, the character-developing and educational aspects of football are meaningless. His players are only a means to his end. They are recruited, paid to play, injected with dreams of pro careers, and generally molded into what is identified as a jock, a person whose whole life revolves around playing a competitive sport (football in this case) and who dreams of becoming a pro star.

Obviously, a coach like this couldn't survive in a college athletic program unless somebody let him. Thus, the university administration must accept some of the responsibility for his presence. Regardless of who takes the blame, the college football programs such coaches direct are in no way small time. Sure, they may be listed in the Small College Division of the NCAA and in the Small College Football Poll, but don't kid yourself—their philosophy is big time all the way.

These examples, Long Beach State and the eastern college, were mentioned to illustrate the fact that many athletic programs that title themselves small college, are only miniature replicas of the overgrown big-time athletic machines. Nevertheless, this does not mean that all small colleges dream big-time athletic thoughts. There are some, although their numbers seem to diminish each year, that operate on a small scale quite happily and successfully, and they may offer a reasonable solution to the athletic machine mess.

Some of the best examples of this group are the colleges that make up the College Conference of Illinois and Wisconsin (CCIW), which consists of Illinois Wesleyan, Augustana, Millikin, Wheaton, Elmhurst, North Central, North Park, Carthage, and Carroll colleges, and the colleges that compose the Southern California Intercollegiate Athletic Association: California Technological Institute, Pomona, Whittier, Redlands, Claremont-Pitzer; Occidental, and LaVerne Colleges.

The schools in both these conferences are small colleges (their enrollments average about 2,000 students per school) with small athletic programs, but by design, not by accident. It would be easy, athletic directors in the leagues intimate, for their programs to be much bigger and emphasized far more, but that's not the desire of the colleges, their conferences, or their coaches.

Most of the coaches are coaching because they enjoy it and the opportunity it presents for them to teach young men, not because they have an incessant desire to win at all costs and to build their fame and future on their win-loss record.

In the College Conference of Illinois and Wisconsin, for instance, the schools are limited in the number of athletic scholarships they can award and the few allowed are based on financial need and academic ability. Thus, an important form of control exists within the CCIW: the force of equal competition. With this form of equal footing it is just a matter of a team's desire to win, its skill, and the breaks, that make the difference between winning and losing records.

Make no mistake, winning is still an important commodity in the CCIW and the competition is fierce. CCIW teams are no slouches either. Several conference teams have beaten larger schools with big athletic programs. For instance, Illinois Wesleyan has experienced great success in baseball recently and

Wheaton College has done likewise in basketball, even though they've both retained their same athletic philosophies.

If you are thinking that major university powers that are in conferences which limit the number of scholarships they can offer, such as the Big Ten with 120 in football, have a similar situation—they all start with an equal footing too, and you're only partially correct. That's where the similarity between the CCIW and big-time conferences ends and the differences begin. The big-time conference schools dream of growing even bigger and are forced to produce a winner in order to draw a big gate and to pay their bills. So they all try to do things in a bigger way than the next guy. CCIW schools know the consequences of such action and instead of striving to get bigger, they fight to keep things small and equal.

It should be mentioned that labeling the CCIW athletic programs as small time is probably a misnomer. More appropriately, their programs should be labeled real college athletics—meaning that their emphasis is on the student and enhancing his personal experience through competitive sports. The emphasis is not on paying athletes, winning games at any cost, filling stadiums, and developing pro prospects, as it is with big athletic powers.

If big-time athletics could ever be retooled and brought back to this sensible small college or real college level, like that which exists in the CCIW and the SCIA conferences, and not like the quasi-small college programs discussed earlier, (Long Beach State and the others listed) it would indeed present another workable solution to today's tarnished athletic machines.

On the East Coast, the Ivy League Conference, consisting of such schools as Yale, Harvard, Dartmouth, Columbia, and the like, is another oft-cited example that approximates real college athletics and which could serve as a model for re-shaping the athletic machine. The conference does, in a sense, operate under an athletic philosophy which is in agreement with the factors (to be discussed in a later section) that constitute true college athletics. The Ivy League Conference requires its member schools to base the award of grant-in-aids on financial need and academic achievement. Schools within the circuit, for the most part, play within their own conference and do not play intersectional games, nor do they accept bids to post-season bowl games.

If there is a weakness within the Ivy League approach to athletics, it lies in the realm of recruitment and coaching. Several coaches within the league recruit athletes as vigorously as do their counterparts in the big-time conferences like the Southeastern and Southwestern, the big Ten and the Pacific Eight. Although the need program and the requirement of academic prowess necessary for entry to their schools serve as strong restraints for their recruiting activity, these eager coaches, most noticeably at Dartmouth and Yale in recent years, have conducted big-time (like athletic recruiting) operations which indicate they lean toward the win-at-all-cost philosophy.

Regardless of this weakness, which has not been great enough over the years to cause the conference to become big-time, the Ivy League and its member schools illustrate a solution to the current athletic mess which is rather consistent with that presented by the College Conference of Illinois and Wisconsin and the California Intercollegiate Athletic Association Conference.

The last solution for dissolving the athletic machine has been peddled through articles in magazines like *Sports Illustrated, Newsweek, Look,* and *Human Behavior,* on the sports pages of newspapers, and in books written by former players who have turned into pious sports critics. The solution suggests reorganizing the control of college athletics so that winning won't be its primary function and that college sports becomes an activity for the students, not just for the coaches, fans, and alumni. Although this cry has been bellowed frequently in the past, today the torch is most gallantly carried by Jack Scott and his workers of the Institute for the Study of Sport and Society. As mentioned in an earlier section, the institute is an athletic and sports reform group originally based in Oakland, California, and now in Oberlin, Ohio, where its originator and spearhead, Jack Scott, is the Athletic Director at Oberlin College. Scott is also the author of the group's two bibles, *Athletics for Athletes* and *The Athletic Revolution,* both of which are dedicated to the subject of returning collegiate athletics to their rightful place, the students.

Other members of the group, like Dave Meggyesy, a former St. Louis Cardinal pro footballer and the author of *Out of My League,* and former New York Jet receiver, George Sauer, support the same thought and have given the movement much publicity.

Members of this fraternity chastise big-time collegiate sports for its inhumane treatment of athletics, the similarity of its coaching methods to the military, for overemphasizing winning, and for its kinship with today's commercial-industrial society where everything must bring a material reward. They aren't exaggerating either; they have ammunition to back up their contentions. For instance, they say that, "Psychologists who have done extensive psychological testing on college coaches have found them to be one of the most authoritarian groups in American society; they often outscore policemen and even career military officers on measures of authoritarianism." The institute and its disciples claim such authoritarianism causes coaches and athletic departments to use their players as gladiators in quest of the hollow glories they hold in such high esteem. They further claim big-time college athletics is just like professional sports, because its players are paid to play and because its games are intended to entertain the public and make money. There's little doubt about the truth of these claims either. Everybody with sense knows college players spend as much time on athletics as their pro counterparts but aren't paid nearly as much. In fact, Jack Scott claims Lew Alcindor (Kareem Abdul Jabbar) once told him (while still at UCLA) that playing for the Milwaukee Bucs would be just like playing for UCLA except he'd be paid $200 grand instead of spending money plus tuition and room and board. Scott also relates that Paul Brechler, former University of California at Berkeley athletic director, proudly told him that the only difference between Cal's football program and that of the San Francisco 49ers was that Cal's football players were college students. But when questioned about the pay difference between Cal's players and the 49ers, Brechler said, "Our boys are amateurs." Of course Scott's group capitalized on Brechler's slip and now employ it to support their slaps at big-time collegiate athletics' hypocrisy and absurdity. And rightfully so!

The irony of college athletes playing for these low wages, even though they are really pros, is that they have no choice, Scott claims. The NCAA restricts college athletes from signing pro contracts until four years after their high school graduation. This rule assures college coaches that their stars will be with them for four seasons and can't be lured away by big pro contracts. Recent early signings with the pros by some collegiate basketball stars prior to playing out their four years (Spencer Haywood from the University of Detroit and Robert McAdoo from the University of North Carolina being the most prominent examples of such in recent years) may alter this situation. Nevertheless, the present rule still forces the players to be at the mercy of the big-time collegiate recruiters and coaches if they wish to continue playing.

After high school graduation, players really have four choices: accept a low paying full ride at some athletic machine for four years, thus serving a pro internship; play in a real college program for fun and possibly give up any pro aspirations; leave the country to play pro ball; or give up the sport altogether. That's what you call a dilemma. Obviously, most athletes accept the full ride and play pro ball at a university for four years. As a result, the NCAA and the big-time powers really are forcing themselves to continue college athletics on a pro scale by maintaining this rule. The pros, particularly football and basketball teams, don't mind though. It saves them the millions of dollars it would cost to develop their own minor leagues, as baseball has done.

The rule has another drawback as well. It forces boys into college whose only reason for going to school is to serve their pro internship.

To further support the Institute for the Study of Sport and Society's contentions concerning college athletics' shortcomings, Mr. Scott, who often mixes a little pseudomarxist philosophy with his thoughts, said, "The present structure of university athletics has destroyed the intrinsic value of sport just as our bureaucratic-industrial society has destroyed the intrinsic value of work. The modern worker—both blue and white collar—finds little self-fulfillment, or self-actualization, through his work. Deriving no satisfaction from his employment, he fetishizes the commodities his work enables him to purchase. As our Madison Avenue advertisers know all too well, modern man gains his identity from the type of car he drives, the kind of shaving cream he uses, the clothes he wears, or any of the other commodities the hucksters can dream up—from anything but his actual work. Athletics can, and should, be a form of self-expression just as a man's work should be an expression of himself. Sadly, the college athlete who is able to find intrinsic value from sport is as rare as the worker who finds it from his employment."

The college athlete's commodity fetish he speaks about is the way naive athletes are misled into identifying with a big-time program, its victories and glories—not with their own development through the joy of playing. "The fetishism of victory so common today," Jack Scott says, "must be stopped. To make victory the only meaning of athletic participation is as restricting as making a woman's boot the sole basis for sexual meaning."

Lastly, Scott says, "In a system of athletics for athletes, students would learn the value of autonomous discipline rather than authoritarian discipline, and they would begin to experience joy from the free but exhausting exercise of their bodies. There would be track meets, basketball games, swimming meets and other games, but the emphasis would be on competence rather than competition. Athletes would be concerned with expressing themselves as well as possible rather than with proving themselves superior to their opponents." If you could remove the thought from college coaches' minds that they are developing players for the pros, this goal would have a chance of becoming reality. Although it appears Mr. Scott is calling for an elimination of scorekeeping in sports, in reality, he is only calling for the placement of winning in its proper perspective. Scott advocates a balance between the cooperative and competitive aspects of sports. He feels that winning is a necessary part of any game, and it is essential that it remain. However, it needs toning down.

Although members of the Institute for the Study of Sport and Society philosophize a lot, their criticisms are very biting and real. So real, in fact, that most coaches only speak of them in whispers and only mention Jack Scott's name when in the privacy of their trophy-lined offices.

Scott and company aren't throwing in collegiate athletics' towel yet, though. They feel college sports can be saved by giving it back to the students. They claim that assigning regular academic teachers to a school's coaching duties, including athletics as part of a school's regular curriculum, and eliminating the commercialism from college athletics would do the job.

Few disagree with the Jack Scott group that college athletics should be an activity for the students, but the problem is how to get it there. One can't help but wonder exactly what Scott and his comrades in the Institute for the Study of Sport and Society really mean by "give the control of the sport back to the athletes" and other such phrases. There could be several interpretations. Thus, this is a reform movement with a direction but no plan for reaching it.

So the third popular solution to the muddle of the athletic machine doesn't supply a complete answer either, although it does give athletic reformers a goal. That goal is to convert collegiate athletics into the student-centered activity it was intended to be but never became. The task is now to chart a course for reaching that goal and to define what is meant by "turning the control of athletics over to the students" and making it an "activity for the students."

There Is an Answer

Now it is time to contemplate an answer to the collegiate athletic mess. To accommodate this purpose, this section will present a program for curing the curses of the athletic machine.

Several factors fostered the development of the athletic machine, as has been previously discussed, but there was one overriding void that allowed these factors to begin operating in the first place. That was the loss of control by university presidents of their schools' athletic programs and its coaches. This loss of control occurred for several reasons: the presidents lacked adequate concern; the alumni exerted pressure on the schools for their presidents and athletic programs to produce winners; and ignorance on the part of the presidents as to what was happening.

Be that as it may, in reality the actual cause is of little importance. What is important, however, is how to

correct the old errors and how to avoid their recur-
rence in the future. Ironically, the only people capable
of making these corrections and regaining control of
intercollegiate athletics are the ones who originally
lost it: the presidents and their boards of trustees.

Thus, if the university presidents and boards of
trustees from universities across the country would
present a plan for accomplishing such, the nation's
collegiate coaches and athletic directors would be
forced to follow along even though they might offer
resistance at first. That is, the coaches and athletic
directors would follow along if there were sufficient
fire power behind the plan. The plan would require
complete commitment and dedication on the part of
the boards of trustees and the presidents. There could
be no allowances for faint-hearted efforts. The presidents and the boards of trustees would need to decide
to reform the athletic machine completely, or to forget
it and continue to be carried along on the shady,
bumpy road of big-time athletics as many have done
and are still doing.

The NCAA at the national level and the various
athletic conferences on the regional level would need
to accept and adopt the presidents' plans. They would
actually be in a position similar to that of the athletic
directors and coaches. They too might offer some
resistance, but they'd soon have to accept the plan
and its reorganization or face ruin. For, unless the conferences and the NCAA have the support of the university presidents and their boards, their existence is
meaningless.

The program to be proposed here is only one of
probably several from which the presidents and their
boards could choose, but for now it is the only one on
the market that is detailed enough to be installed in the

immediate future and realistic enough to retain the strong points of the present system. Most other plans call for the present system's total ruin, including discarding all its remnants, of which some are worth saving. As a result, this program is offered as the answer.

The total program, as outlined here, consists of six phases which are arranged chronologically so as to make presidents, boards of trustees, and other concerned individuals aware of the following two items: the magnitude of the problem (covered by Phase I) and a means of implementing the plan in the near future (covered in Phases II–VI).

The Program

Phase I

The initial step in any program of change is recognition of the need for change. People, including those from the university communities where big-time athletic programs exist and the general public, must be made aware of the situation as it now stands in collegiate athletics. A book like this is of some help, but it cannot do the entire job. Those who will read it will be aware of the situation to a degree already, and thus, the book's prime function for them will be to solidify their conviction that athletics are in need of change. To publicize the need for change to others, however, information citing examples of collegiate athletic's abuses and wrongdoings will need to be made public by other means.

Such a public disclosure, or publicity program if you will, would not be dissimilar at all to the recent campaigns conducted to make the public aware of such things as the plight of American POWs during the Vietnam crisis; the state of the earth's ecological

imbalance; the unwillingness of automobile manufacturers to concern themselves with safety as cham-
pioned by Ralph Nader; corruption in Congress; or the
recognition that some prized animal species may soon
become extinct unless protected by law.

With those thoughts in mind, it is proposed that a
National Awareness Program for Collegiate Athletic
Reform (NAP-CAR) be arranged to coordinate such a
publicity program. The group's goals would be: to
solicit individuals to work for the cause; to generate
the necessary funding for the advertising campaign;
and to publicize athletic's problems through speeches,
newspaper ads and articles, magazine articles and in-
formative pamphlets especially designed for particular groups, such as university administrators, faculty,
and students, as well as for the general public. A secondary goal, which would be subsequent to the successful completion of the primary goals, would be to
spearhead the various phases of a program similar to
the one presented in the latter portion of this chapter.
This goal, in a sense, would be the adhesive that
would bind and guide all interested parties toward accomplishing the purpose of rerouting intercollegiate
athletics.

Any individual or group could organize and lead
such a coalition (NAP-CAR) but one with some financial resources would probably help make its early
days free from trouble. Nonetheless, interest and
diligence would be the qualities of utmost importance.

Phase II

NAP-CAR would send a letter describing the rationale
for reforming big-time collegiate athletics and a plan
for doing so to the presidents and the chairmen of the

boards of trustees of all the big-time athletic universities in the country, or at least to a good portion of
those from each section of the country. The letter
should ask them to consider the present athletic mess
and the need to reorganize it. It would ask them to
consider the means of doing such clean-up work, particularly as outlined in this program. This same purpose could be accomplished through personal contacts as well. Regardless of the means, however, the
message needs to be brought to the presidents and
their boards.

Hopefully, this original contract would cause the
topic of intercollegiate athletic reform to appear on
the agenda of a forthcoming board of trustees' meeting. At least one of those present at such a meeting
should agree that big-time athletics do need reform.
Hopefully, some of those would be cognizant of and
agree with NAP-CAR's position. It would be best if
several would feel likewise, especially the chairman of
the board and the university president, since they have
the greatest influence—but one supporter at this point
would be sufficient.

A brief questionnaire should be enclosed along
with the letter to the presidents and the boards asking
their opinion of the need to reroute big-time athletics.
These questionnaires should be completed after
athletic reform has been discussed at a board meeting. Once these opinion forms were returned and
tabulated, NAP-CAR would have a strong indication of
the amount of sympathy generated by the program and
the names of those who would be willing to meet
further and discuss athletic reform in more detail.

If the topic of rerouting intercollegiate athletics
and the program advocated here were placed on the

board's agenda, it is with the hope the presidents' and trustees' discussions would include the desire and feasibility of installing such a program and plan at their school, the feasibility of convincing others across the country to do the same and a decision to respond positively to the questionnaire.

Phase III

After the presidents and their boards have had time to consider and discuss the proposals made by letter or personal contact and completed the questionnaire, summit meetings of university presidents, or their representatives, from schools with big-time athletic programs should be arranged. Ideally, these meetings would be set up jointly by NAP-CAR and the interested president and board members. The first battery of these meetings should be at the state or conference level. At this meeting, those involved could discuss the big-time athletic system as it now exists and the ways of correcting it. Ideally, they would agree to regulate and control their own overgrown athletic programs so they could become an activity for the students rather than an entertainment trying to compete with the spectacle of professional sports.

At this point, they'd need to define what is meant by an activity for the students. The following definition is suggested:

Athletics should be a sports program conducted for the students and regulated by the universities through their athletic departments. The program should be conducted according to the student body's desires, interests, and needs. To assure this, students should have a hand in operating the program.

It seems feasible that athletics could be controlled by an athletic board at each university. These boards should be tripartite in nature, consisting of an equal number of students, faculty (a certain percentage of which should be coaches), and administrators. Each member should have one vote and the membership should be rotated on the same basis as is the United States Senate. That way no member or faction of members could control the group for a long period of time. One athletic administrator, the athletic director, would be a permanent member due to his occupational role.

The major responsibility of this group would be to develop athletic policy and goals and to serve as a personnel committee for the selection of the athletic department staff (coaches, administrators, and so forth). They could also serve as a regulating group, dealing with major departmental problems.

Under such an athletic board arrangement, the university would still ultimately control its own athletic program, it would not be exclusively student operated as are club sports programs at some universities.

Although the athletic board arrangement is not new, the majority of all universities currently have one or something quite similar, under this new program they would have administrative authority and not be solely advisory as they are now. They would, in a sense, operate the athletic program.

An activity conducted for the students should also mean that every coach be dedicated to providing an atmosphere in which student learning can be emphasized above all else. It should be an activity in which the students can develop themselves intellectually, socially, and effectively (develop wholesome values and attitudes), and where these goals would be attainable regardless of a team's win-loss record. Winning should be part of such a program but not overemphasized above sports' other values.

Individual honesty, loyalty, and group togetherness, development of an individual's ability to interact with others, players' involvement in team and individual decisions, allowance for individuals to express themselves through the medium of physical activity, and the opportunity for all to reach toward their individual potential, as ultimately defined by themselves, should be stressed.

Another of the athletic board's duties would be to supervise the occurrence of such goals.

Hopefully, delegates at these state or conference level meetings would agree that the first step in instituting such a sports program would be for the presidents never to demand that a coach, or allow the alumni or outside pressures to demand that a coach, produce a winner.

Obviously, there would need to be several other points of agreement too, but regardless of whether the ultimate purpose of total agreement were accomplished at these state and conference level meetings, I hope that the major outcome would be of interest to the various representatives so that they will meet with delegates from other similar meetings held throughout the country. If so, another phase would be necessary.

Phase IV

The next summit meetings should be held on the regional level. Hopefully, the presidents or their delegates from the first meetings would see merit in, and a method for, athletic reform and attend the regional meeting.

For those who did not agree at the state meeting and did not feel another meeting was necessary, hopefully, they would still send a representative or at least agree to read a transcript of the proceedings.

The object of these second meetings should be to have the presidents and their representatives from each region of the country agree that reform is necessary and thus lend support and reassurance to each other that they should continue in their quest to turn big-time athletics around. This agreement would satisfy the minimum goal of the meeting. The maximum goal would be for all to agree to institute an athletic reform program like the one presented here, or something very similar. Exact agreement with the program and its plan, as presented here, however, is not necessary to achieve the maximum goal but agreement to something similar is mandatory.

A regional meeting should be held in the South, Midwest, and on the East and West Coasts. Optimally at this point, the leadership would have shifted from the hands of NAP-CAR to those of the presidents, their boards, and their representatives.

Phase V

It may be necessary for yet another round of conferences, this time at the national level. Such a conference should consist of elected representatives from the various regional meetings. Its primary purpose should be to formally sign a national coalition to regulate big-time college athletics and return them to their rightful position. The secondary purpose of this meeting should be to organize a permanent athletic control board and to elect board members from each regional group.

Phase VI

The next phase would be convening the first meeting of the athletic control board organized at the national meeting described in Phase V. The board's function would be to reiterate the need for reforming and controlling college athletics and to formulate policy (from the suggestions of the various summit meetings) and to reinforce the procedures by which it is to be accomplished. It would serve an evaluative purpose too. The board would evaluate the plan's success to date and suggest any necessary adjustments. Its role would not be one of regulating and policing the plan; that duty would be the responsibility of the various schools and their conference commissioners.

The athletic control board would meet annually, at least for the first few years, and would be made up of elected regional university presidents or their representatives, of which no voting members could be affiliated with university athletic departments.

The Plan

Following are the suggested items that the presidents and the boards would need to discuss and ideally agree upon during Phases IV, V, and VI. Even though some of the items are more detailed than others, most are stated in general terms. However, they are only intended to serve as guideposts around which more detailed plans can be constructed later, if need be.

The plan is divided into two parts.

I. Reform Measures

A. Require that the intercollegiate athletic program be financed through a student activities budget and/or the regular university budget. The control of the budget allotted to athletics would ultimately be under the auspices of the athletic board whose on-the-job representative would be the athletic director. Of course, the athletic board would be answerable to the university president.

B. Require that all income from intercollegiate athletics, such as game receipts, radio or TV rights, etc., go directly into the student activities fund or the regular university budget and not into athletic departments or into one single sport's coffer. These receivable funds would be combined with all other sources of income and given to the student activities council or the university budget office and would, in part, determine the following year's budgets, including that of athletics. Obviously, the greater the revenues, the greater next year's budget for all areas, not just athletics.

C. Require that all athletic scholarships be renamed *activity scholarship grants* and awarded through the university's student financial aid office. Make the awarding of these grants contingent upon meeting the standard entrance requirements of the university and upon the student's need for financial assistance to attend college. The same title, activity scholarship grants, should apply to other student activity grants, such as for band, orchestra, and debate. The same procedure of need employed when awarding all other university scholarships should be utilized for awarding activity scholarship grants. The university student financial aid office should control the award of all such scholarships. The athletic departments would simply be able to inform prospective athletes how to go about seeking aid, they would not be able to influence the financial aid office to give certain applicants awards unless they were deemed qualified by that office. The student financial aid offices, in other words, would no longer be just rubber stamps for athletic scholarships, but would actually make the decisions concerning who is to receive financial aid as they do for other students.

D. Restrict the number of activity scholarships available for athletics. The following formulas are suggested means by which this could be done. The first of these is to limit the number of activity scholarship grants, totally (for four years), for each sport to the number of players on the various sports teams, such as football—11, basketball—5, baseball—9, track—9, etc., etc. The numbers mentioned could be altered— these are only suggestions. Remember these figures represent the number available totally for each sport, not just for one year. The second possible formula would be to limit activity grants to ten percent of the number of players on a team. For instance, football grants equal 10 percent x 11 = 1.1 per year or 4½ totally; basketball grants equal 10 percent x 5 = .5 per year or 2 totally for four years. Although the suggested formulas are built around the number of players in the various sports, there no doubt are several other equally good formulas or methods. The grants within each sport could be subdivided in any manner. One player's grant could include tuition, another only fees, another room and board, and still another, book allowance. In fact, this practice should be encouraged so there would be few, if any, players on full grants.

E. Restrict the recruitment of athletes to within the boundaries of the state in which the university is located. The athletic board would play the key role in assuring the success of this proposal since they would control the budget—they would only approve travel and expense money for in-state recruitment.

F. Restrict the amount of money that could be used for recruitment to a minimal amount each year, everything included, such as travel, meals, and telephone bills. A figure such as $5,000 is suggested. Obviously, this figure is only hypothetical but it is mentioned to illustrate the drastic cut that this program would make in funds available for recruitment. Some schools, as indicated earlier, spend in the hundreds of thousands of dollars on this project now.

G. Prohibit the athletic department or friends of the athletic department from financing a prospective athlete's visit to the campus. If a prospect wishes to visit the campus, then he must finance it himself. Restricting the athletic department's involvement in such activity would be simple, as described under item E, but doing likewise for the so-called friends of the athletic department would be difficult. Again, supervision by the athletic board would be the key. Publicizing the school's athletic policy concerning such matters to booster clubs and the like would be the first step. Reprimanding any school personnel or refusing admissions to any prospective athletes involved would be another necessary measure. Once the word got around, due to publicity and/or a few trial reprimands, the incidence of outsiders participating in athletics in this fashion would subside greatly. Another major problem in regard to friends is their frequent offers of under-the-table financial assistance to prospective or current athletes. This issue could be handled in the same manner as the control of free trips to visit universities. Tight restrictions and definite consequences would be mandatory, particularly as related to the athletes or university personnel involved in or even aware of such situations.

H. Limit coaching staffs for each sport. For example, 4 for football, 2 for basketball, etc., and require the coaches to be a part of the regular faculty and perform teaching or other commensurate duties during the off-season. Once again, the budget control exercised by the athletic board would allow for restraint in this area. If the number of coaches is to be limited as indicated, every effort would need to be exerted to employ the best coaches possible, particularly in regard to athletic and educational philosophy and agreement with these suggested restrictions. Their expertise in the sport they coach and their ability to communicate successfully would also be of great importance. United States International University, a small liberal arts college in California, recently sought to employ a new football coach. They sent the following information and indirect job description to all applicants with the idea of making their athletic policy quite clear to all candidates and to assure their employing the best person to fit their needs. Such an approach may provide a rather simple means of solving many of today's current athletic problems.

"We at United States International University," said athletic director Dr. Norris Patterson, "are looking for a teacher-coach to fill our vacancy as football coach. We are looking for someone who will accept the school's plans to switch the recruiting priority from junior colleges to high schools, to eliminate spring practice and to compete on the same level as other private schools.

"What we're doing starting in '74," said Patterson, "is altering our schedule. We won't be playing schools like Los Angeles State, UC-Riverside or Cal Poly Pomona anymore. We'll compete on the same level as the Southern California Intercollegiate Athletic Conference—schools like Pomona, Redlands, Whittier, Cal Tech. They're small private schools like us.

"It's important that we have someone familiar with the high schools and junior colleges in California. But recruiting is not that important. All our grants are based on need; we don't give athletic scholarships. We're not in the recruiting business. If we recruited heavily and put a lot of money into our program we would run ourselves out of business. The last thing we want to do is drop football."

I. Restrict organized practice to the regular season and one month prior. Eliminate such things as year 'round football programs including spring drills.

J. Prohibit separate living quarters, training tables, and special registration for athletes and other groups.

K. Establish and enforce academic eligibility standards for athletic and other activity groups.

L. Resolve to release any faculty member, coach, or athletic director from his duties upon involvement and responsibility in the violation of one of these prescribed rules and policies. As indicated, the athletic board would shoulder this burden.

M. All booster club or alumni funds given to the university must go directly into the student activity fund or university foundation and cannot be given directly to the athletic department or to any one sport for a particular purpose within that sport.

N. Limit each athletic team to one intersectional game (outside of their region, Midwest, South, etc.) every two years.

II. Regulating the Plan

A. Agree that each university and its president would restrict and control its own athletic program as outlined in the plan. This duty would require a special committee (the athletic board), which would be directly responsible to the president and not to the athletic department. Each school's guidelines for regulating itself should be submitted to the national athletic control board for approval.

B. Agree that the athletic conferences should be partially charged with regulating and supervising policies of the plan on a regional level and their commissioners should be directly responsible to the university presidents. Jointly, the conferences should set up guidelines for accomplishing their task. This could best be done by having the conferences nation-wide and involved in developing and approving such guidelines. The various conference plans would need to be approved on the national level by the athletic control board. The conference's regulating group would need to work closely with each school's athletic board.

C. Independent universities, those not in the con-ferences, would each be regulated by their president and his athletic board. On the regional level, however, they would be controlled and supervised by a commis-sioner of independent programs whose duties would be identical to those of the conference commis-sioners.

D. A national organization, such as the NCAA, would revert back to its original purpose of promoting collegiate athletics in its rightful place and organizing and administering national championship events. They would not be involved in the regulation of recruitment and scholarship violations as they are today.

Many athletic reformers will disagree with some of the proposals in this plan. In particular, they will dis-agree on athletic scholarships, or activity scholarship grants for athletics issue. Many people feel that restriction of athletics means complete elimination of grants-in-aid. There is a need for the availability of grants for athletics, however, as well as a need for comparable scholarships in other activities, such as orchestra, theater, and art. It seems reasonable that college prospects who excel in activities such as these and who possess an above-average academic record should be able to receive a scholarship based jointly upon excellence in these areas.

There will also be complaints in regard to the number of activity scholarship grants available for each sport, but the number of activity scholarship grants made available by the proposed formula are quite ample, if not excessive.

Therefore, if the complaints become too strong, the presidents may decide to eliminate grants for athletics completely. Remember, this is a plan for arranging college athletics so they become games for students to play and enjoy. Anyone who wants them to be something else, such as the spectator spectacles they now are, and does not agree with the plan, should not have anything to do with college athletics after the reform takes place.

Some will question the allotment of money for recruiting. "If this plan is to make athletics real and not big time", some will ask, "what is the need for any recruiting money, since coaches will no longer be 'beating the bushes' for athletes or paying them to play?" It's true, the idea is to change big-time college sports and remake them into the real college athletics played by students that they were originally intended to be. But just as universities and their various departments should attempt to interest good students in attending their schools by making their programs known, so should schools' athletic programs attempt to do the same.

Possibly, these two purposes could be accomplished jointly. When a university sends its representatives out to high schools and junior colleges to speak at special events and college nights, perhaps the school's athletic department could be represented at the same time.

Scorners will also attack the program in its entirety because of the impracticality for presidents from all the big-time athletic powers to get together. No doubt it would be a big problem too. Nevertheless, if people want to do something bad enough they will find a way. If the presidents feel that big-time college athletics present a big enough problem—and many of them do—hopefully, they'll be eager to meet and discuss the subject.

All of the attacks mentioned will be voiced, but there is one that will be shouted louder than the rest. The complaint will be that even if such a plan were installed, it would be impossible to police. It would be too, if people's attitudes toward athletics do not change along with the makeup of big-time athletics. The key to the policing issue is to have only those people involved with athletics who support and believe in the reform. In other words, the coaches, athletic directors, university presidents, and conference commissioners will all need to be believers. All of today's big-time coaches and recruiters who refuse to change their attitude and believe, or at least to have an open mind toward the new plan and to give it a chance, must be replaced.

If expecting to change people's minds overnight sounds like a dream to you, you are right. However, if you support your opinion by saying it will be impossible to have a pure sports program in a corrupt, impure world—you are wrong. It can be done. But those who wish to accomplish it had better be adequately dedicated and committed to the cause and ready to face all kinds of opposition. If they are all of these things, and are ready to combat the scoffers and gradually surround themselves with other believers, they will eventually succeed in transforming their dream into reality. How long will all this take? Who knows? But a good guess would be five years for a complete reversal of the athletic machine, if the reform movement were started today.

Obviously, the particular details concerning each item in the plan would need to be worked out prior to its implementation. Nevertheless, the plan provides an adequate framework around which workable details can be constructed. It could and should be implemented immediately, at least Phases II–IV concerning the initial contact with the university presidents of the big-time athletic schools.

The meetings are the key to the success of the whole plan. If the presidents meet and resolve to dismantle the athletic machine which, by the way, would not be an easy resolution for certain presidents because of alumni pressures and their school's big-time athletic tradition, setting up procedures for implementing the plan would be comparatively easy.

Section I of part II would be one of the most difficult sections of the entire operation to develop. Presidents of big-time universities and conference representatives would need to meet regularly for a period of time to develop procedures for regulating the president's policies. The NCAA, with its experience in the regulation of collegiate athletics could be of great assistance to the conference commissioners, the presidents, the athletic control board, and the various athletic boards in suggesting successful methods.

As mentioned before, people's attitudes toward the plan will be the key to policing it. Above all, if the presidents, the conferences, the athletic directors, and the coaches could place the welfare of the students uppermost in their minds when considering these radical changes, the task would be much simpler. That, however, is a big order.

In their big-time athletic thoughts, those people have given students a back seat for so long that it will be hard for them to change. In fact, some scorners will cast the whole program aside for just that reason. "How," they will say, "does anyone think they are going to alter the big-time athletic thoughts of the presidents from athletic machine schools like those in Texas, Alabama, Ohio, and California, let alone the at attitude of their respective coaches?"

Very simply—by forgetting the latter and concentrating on the former. Many big-time coaches are beyond hope and must be sidetracked. Their presidents however, are not. Any educator with concern for students certainly has considered such a reform at one time or another, although he may not publicly admit it. Giving the idea a passing thought in the privacy of one's mind is quite different from making a total public commitment to it, however. It is even more difficult to make that commitment all alone. Thus, to make this easier, the presidents need to rally the support of the other presidents and schools with similar feelings. This program offers an avenue through which this can be done. When presidents from around the country do meet to discuss big-time athletic reform, they will probably be pleasantly surprised to discover how many other presidents share their thoughts.

Just because they have wholesome thoughts, however, does not mean they will be protected from pressures to retain the big-time status quo. Alumni like big programs because of the prestige it gives the old alma mater. Coaches like them because of the ego trip it provides and the pros like them because it provides a cheap and readily available farm league. And there are other special interest groups with their own reasons for keeping things as they are. They will all try to force their influence upon the presidents to bend in their favor. No doubt these groups will exert direct and indirect pressure upon the presidents through national associations, their legislators, big university donors, and other sources available. But the presidents must ward off these scorners and become, in a sense, untouchable. With a complete commitment, they will overcome the pressures and succeed.

Once the state or conference meetings are convened, as outlined in Phase II, and the presidents have made their initial commitment and stated their resolutions, the contest will become a one-sided one. So, it could be said to presidents, "Open your minds and prepare to clean up the immorality, uselessness, cheating, and lack of purpose, characteristic of today's intercollegiate athletic machines."

The basic premise underlying this entire program is that there is a need to save collegiate athletics; that they are inherently good, but not as they exist today. There is a need to destroy the present system insofar as its useless parts are concerned and create a new one to replace it. As you probably have gathered from reading this book, the destruction process is already under way and the machine is crumbling by itself under pressure of its overweight budgets, illegal recruiting practices, and its neglect of individual respect.

The really big problem is how to dismantle it in such a way that a new collegiate sports program, molded around the students' interests, can be constructed from remnants of the old one. The program presented in this book should assure the quickest and easiest possible transition between that breakdown and the rebuilding process.

Thus, as indicated, it is presented as the answer.

Index

A

155

bowl games, 27
budgets, university, 15
foundations, 20
gate receipts, 14
state appropriations, 15
TV, 25
Florida A & M University, 87
Florida, University of, 22, 35, 44
Fordham University, 112
Free ride, 65–81,141–42

G

Gaither, Jake, 87
Game of the Week, 7
Georgia Institute of Technology, 5, 14, 32, 35
Georgia, University of, 26, 28
Georgetown University, 112
Green, Robert L., 102–3

H

Hass, Walter, 112
Hayes, Woody, 5, 95–96
Haywood, Spencer, 126
Hill, Jess, 12, 79
Houston, University of, 6
Howard, Frank, 14

I

Illinois State University, 20, 117
Illinois, University of
    at Champaign, 5, 16–17, 21, 35, 58–60
    at Chicago Circle, 25
Illinois Wesleyan College, 121–22

Indiana University, 102
Institute for the Study of Sport and Society, 124–29
Iowa State University, 28, 33, 69
Ireland, George, 92
Ivy League, 123–24

J

Jabbar, Kareem Abdul, 6, 57, 125
Jackson, Kerry, 51–54
Jacksonville University, 6
Joliet Junior College, 53

K

Kansas State University, 44, 90
Kansas, University of, 18–19
Kentucky, University of, 33

L

Laney Junior College, 53
La Mar, Dwight, 61
LaVerne College, 121
Los Angeles Rams, 117
Louisiana State University, 12–13
Louisiana Tech., 117
Loyola University, Chicago, 92
Loyola University of Los Angeles, 109–14
Lutz, Peter, 72

M

MacAdoo, Robert, 126
McAllister, James, 49–51, 75
McLard, Bill, 47

McClure, Tim, 45–46, 85, 95
McKay, John, 79
McMillian, Joseph, 102
Majors, Johnny, 33
Meat on the Hoof, 86
Meggyesy, Dave, 124
Miami-Dade Junior College, 53
Miami, University of, at Florida, 10, 21, 33, 57
Michigan State University, 32–33
Michigan, University of, 36
Midwest Conference, 69
Millikin College, 121
Minnesota, University of,
      at Duluth, 116
      at Minneapolis, 13
Mississippi, University of, 16, 58
Missouri, University of, 57
Montana, University of, 76
Morgan State College, 97
Mormon church, 5

N

Nassau Community College, 53
National Association of Basketball Coaches, 60
National Awareness Program for Collegiate Athletic Reform
      (NAP-CAR), 134–39
National Collegiate Athletic Association (NCAA), 10, 26, 27,
      29, 31–32, 36, 40, 42–43, 48–49, 54, 60, 63,
      75–82, 115–18, 120, 126, 132, 147, 150
National Football League (NFL), 24, 58
Nebraska, University of, 13, 33, 47, 69
Nevada, University of, at Las Vegas, 34
New Mexico State University, 61, 97
New Mexico, University of, 4–5, 15, 45
New Orleans Saints, 24

Stanford University, 40, 45, 85
Stowell, Joe, 6
Sugar Bowl, 28

T

Tarkanian, Jerry, 34
Tennessee, University of, 26
Texas, University of, 16, 27, 33, 86
Tulane University, 24
Tutko, Thomas A., 88–89, 94

U

United States International University, 144–45

V

Villanova University, 13, 33

W

Wall, Bill, 60–65
Washington, University of, 6, 87, 101–5
West Texas State University, 117
Westchester State University, 117
Western Athletic Conference (WAC), 56
Western Kentucky, University of, 61
Wheaton College, 121–22
Wheeler, Mark, 87
Whittier College, 121
Wisconsin, University of, 113
Wooden, John, 5

Y

Yale College, 24, 45, 123

About the Author

Dr. Evans is chairman of the physical education and athletic department and coordinator of graduate studies in physical education at United States International University, Elliot Campus, San Diego, California.

He has lived in a college sports atmosphere all his life, for his father was athletic director at Northern Illinois University for thirty-nine years. Dr. Evans, during his intercollegiate days, played on championship football teams and later coached various sports at both high school and college levels.

After earning his B.S. and M.S. degrees at Northern Illinois University, he earned an Ed.D. degree at the University of New Mexico.

The author is also an authority on physical education and sports for children at the elementary school level, and at the present time is writing a book on motor skill learning.